GARDENS OF
THE NORTH SHORE
OF CHICAGO

GARDENS OF THE NORTH SHORE OF CHICAGO

BENJAMIN F. LENHARDT JR.

PHOTOGRAPHS BY SCOTT SHIGLEY

THE MONACELLI PRESS

CONTENTS

FOREWORD

Barbara Whitney Carr

Sheridan Road runs the entire length of Chicago's North Shore—meandering some twenty miles along the shore of Lake Michigan from the edge of the city through one bucolic residential suburb to another, each as green and charming as the last. The views throughout this journey to the end of Chicago's northern suburbs are an almost unbroken ribbon of houses and gardens that generations of Chicagoans have enjoyed since the early summer homes and great estates were built along the "North Shore" in the late nineteenth century. Surely Sheridan Road is one of the most scenic suburban thoroughfares in the world, and it serves as an apt introduction to the gardens that are tucked behind those views, mile on mile.

I was first driven up Sheridan Road as a child of eight when my family was relocating from the city to our new home in the northern suburbs, and I still remember with extraordinary clarity that the ride was as pretty a drive as I had seen in my short life. It is still that today. Now, in hindsight, I find it strange and mystifying that no book was written about the beautiful gardens of Chicago's North Shore in all these years. Perhaps such a well-kept secret awaited the keen eye and curious mind of Ben Lenhardt. He has spent the past three years assembling the stories of garden owners and garden makers to accompany spectacular photographs by Scott Shigley of their North Shore gardens, a collection worth waiting for.

I met Ben and his wife, Cindy, early on during the dozen years I served as President and CEO of the Chicago Botanic Garden, when Ben was invited to serve on the Board of the Garden. Ben was a financier, but in whatever spare time he had throughout those years, he developed his great love for gardens and gardening and no small amount of expertise along the way. He has gardened both in Winnetka, Illinois, and Charleston, South Carolina, visited gardens all over the world, and became the highly respected Chairman of the Garden Conservancy for seven years. During that time, he championed the importance of preserving great gardens and of ensuring that American gardens be shared with the public as broadly as possible.

So finally, indeed: the author with his love of gardening and expert eye, trained through years of viewing gardens throughout the world, has written about the beautiful gardens of various styles and sizes on Chicago's North Shore. Seldom has the time seemed better to match the right man to the assignment and to welcome Ben's collection of North Shore gardens that so many of us have been waiting to see unveiled.

Ben once told me, "Great gardens have souls." *Gardens of the North Shore of Chicago* is a collection of exceptional gardens that Ben has ensured are gardens with souls— all reflecting the visions of the people who dreamed of them and the people who made them.

INTRODUCTION

Magnificent gardens are living works of art. Preserving these ephemeral creations is incredibly challenging as they require remaining true to their design origins, continual evaluation and maintenance, and face threats from natural forces. As Russell Page, the legendary landscape designer, observed, "There are few gardens that can be left alone. A few years of neglect and only the skeleton of a garden can be traced."

In many cases—perhaps most—documenting them is the best way significant gardens can be preserved for future generations. Documenting outstanding American gardens is one of the programs of the Garden Conservancy, the national nonprofit organization of which I had the pleasure of serving as chairman. Over the last three years, I have worked to record the essence of exceptional gardens on the North Shore of Chicago, an area where I have lived and gardened for many years. I also wanted to show the creativity, diversity, and beauty of gardens in the Chicago area, a region not well publicized for its gardening talents. This book is the culmination of that effort. Photographer Scott Shigley has captured the beauty and atmosphere of the gardens through his lens, and his images will become part of the Garden Conservancy's archives.

Before the earliest European explorers reached the Chicago area in the late seventeenth century, the land was occupied by Pottawatomi Indians. Their native landscape consisted of hardwood forest, savanna, open prairie, and marshland. Close to Lake Michigan was a hardwood forest, with oak varieties being predominant. The towering oaks provided shade for a lower story of small trees and shrubs, and the forest floor was covered with wildflowers and moss.

West of the lake were oak savannas that opened up to tallgrass prairie characterized by gentle hills and vast stretches of flatland leading to the Great Plains. Prairie vegetation consisted primarily of grasses that grew as tall as six to ten feet high by August. These grasses were interspersed with shorter grasses, summer wildflowers, and prairie roses.

The term "North Shore" generally refers to the eight autonomous suburbs north of Chicago stretching twenty-two miles from Evanston north to Lake Bluff. These suburbs—Evanston, Wilmette, Kenilworth, Winnetka, Glencoe, Highland Park, Lake Forest and Lake Bluff—were incorporated between 1857 to 1896. Some of the names of these villages and towns relate to their landscapes. For example, Lake Forest derived its name from Lake Michigan and the forest initially found there; Lake Bluff from the bluffs above the lake; and Winnetka from a Native American word meaning "beautiful land." Each North Shore community has its own character, but all share a beautiful Lake Michigan shoreline, lake breezes, and close proximity to the great city of Chicago.

Above: Crab Tree Farm.

The North Shore's dominant topographical features are Lake Michigan and a series of ancient ravines. Lake Michigan, third-largest of the Great Lakes, is 365 miles long and is of varying depths up to 870 feet. The shoreline is a smooth curve without bays or promontories. From Winnetka to Lake Bluff, ravines are found in a narrow band along the shore. These ravines were created nearly 12,000 years ago when the last glaciers of the Ice Age melted, forming streams that eroded the earth as they flowed toward the lake. Today, these ravines are significant landscape features and have created unique plant and animal communities.

Gardening on the North Shore is challenging. The growing season is short— May through September; the soil is predominantly clay; and the weather is extremely variable. Summers are warm, humid, and wet with the average high temperature in the mid 80s, while winters are frigid and windy with the average low temperature in the mid 20s. Unfortunately, the low and high temperatures can vary significantly from the averages. In 2019, the low temperature was -29 and the high was 98, which can be stressful and sometimes devastating to plants.

Railroading was an essential factor in the growth of Chicago and the North Shore, particularly the Chicago and North Western Railroad established in 1866. These trains provided frequent, on-time, and inexpensive transportation to and from

Above: Bluhm Garden.

Right: Camp Rosemary.

Chicago to North Shore communities, allowing residents to live on the bucolic North Shore and work in downtown Chicago and commute to the city for shopping and entertainment.

Chicago was the fastest growing city in America in the last quarter of the nineteenth century. Expanding businesses and new residents began to encroach on the enclaves of the rich who lived on Prairie Avenue and other parts of Chicago's wealthy South Side. For many, a move to the North Shore was the solution—it offered everything—a magnificent landscape and lakefront, spaciousness, and a gracious lifestyle.

Noted architects, landscape architects, and designers were hired to create substantial North Shore estates for Chicago industrialists, bankers, merchants, and commodity brokers, primarily in Lake Bluff, Lake Forest and Winnetka. Architects such as Charles A. Platt, Howard Van Doren Shaw, David Adler, Arthur Heun, Harrie T. Lindeberg, Edwin H. Clark, Samuel Marx, and Delano & Aldrich designed houses in the Georgian, arts and crafts, and Beaux-Arts styles for their sophisticated clients. Developing vast landscapes and gardens for these properties in the picturesque and romantic styles were equally well-known landscape architects and designers, including Frederick Law Olmsted, Ellen Biddle Shipman, Warren Manning, Rose Standish Nichols, Jens Jensen, Ossian C. Simmonds, Ferruccio Vitale, and Ralph Root. Due to residential development and the expense of maintaining these estates, few, or only portions of these estates, exist today.

Selecting the gardens to include in this book was not an easy task as there are many unique and beautiful gardens on the North Shore. The common theme running through these gardens is the keen interest the owners have in their paradises. Some owners are "dirt gardeners," while others are less so, but all share a passion and love for their gardens.

The gardens reflect a sensitivity of place and respect for the architecture of the house. The planting and design choices are varied. Some have showy, colorful beds

while others are light and dreamy with drifts of colorful flowers blending one to another. Some are highly structured, formal and perfectly balanced with topiaries and manicured lawns, while others have evolved over time without a specific plan. Others depict Midwestern woodlands and prairies. No matter what the style, plantings, or size of each garden, all share excellence in design and horticulture.

This book includes a few of the extant North Shore estate gardens, but it primarily shows gardens created over the last forty years by owners or with the assistance of prominent landscape architects or designers. I have had the pleasure of knowing many of these owners and their gardens over the years. For others, it has been an opportunity for me to develop new friendships.

The book presents twenty-four private gardens from Winnetka to Lake Bluff and west to Mettawa. Because of its unique design and beauty, one garden, "a little further North" in Fredonia, Wisconsin, has been included. These gardens have been grouped by style into chapters entitled Classic Gardens, Contemporary Gardens, Country Gardens, and Naturalistic Gardens. Few of the gardens have been published, and it is a pleasure to introduce these outstanding landscapes.

A book about outstanding gardens on Chicago's North Shore would not be complete without the Chicago Botanic Garden. The Botanic Garden has inspired many gardeners in this book and has contributed to the high quality of private gardens on the North Shore.

This endeavor has been a joy for me over the last three years as I have focused on my lifelong passion—gardening. After learning the stories of these gardeners and viewing their handiwork, I hope each reader will share my enthusiasm and appreciation for the creators and the works of art they have produced. As Francis Bacon, the English philosopher, said, "God Almighty first planted a garden, and indeed it is the purest of pleasures, it is the greatest refreshment of the spirit of man."

Left: The Rumsey Estate.

Above: Kelton House Farm.

CLASSIC GARDENS

HARRIS GARDEN

WINNETKA

After Caryn and King Harris purchased a
house in Winnetka, their friend John Bryan
recommended Virginia landscape architect
Charles Stick as the designer of the garden
for their new home. This was the beginning
of a long and close relationship with a new
"gardening friend."

On her travels, Caryn Harris always visited
gardens and kept a file on those she found
most interesting. When she and Stick began
to discuss the style of garden she preferred,
her "garden files" confirmed that English-style
gardens were her favorites.

Knowing that the residence would be
occupied mostly during the summer, Stick sought to create a verdant rural
atmosphere to contrast with the Harrises' Chicago life. He surrounded the house
with English country-style designs, using tall yew hedges to create garden rooms.
As Stick explains, "I designed the garden from inside the house looking out."

White-flowering crab apple trees and doublefile viburnum along the entrance drive
create a green-and-white welcoming rhythm. The house is partially clad in climbing
hydrangea and adorned with Regency-style urns that sit atop a Palladian-inspired
hall window parapet. Globe-shaped boxwoods bounded with a low hedge and
grass perimeter dominate the roundabout while larger box spheres and cones flank
the bluestone doorway. For hedges, as well as punctuation, meticulously pruned
boxwood plays a significant role throughout the garden.

On the east side of the house, Stick elegantly threaded a series of garden rooms
together. Guests moving through the spaces feel a sense of discovery to explore the
next delight. Box hedging and bluestone paving contribute to harmony throughout
the garden. A rose garden, with its yew walls and box parterres, is in bloom from
late spring to fall with David Austin roses in Caryn's favorite shades of pink, coral,
and white. Climbing hydrangea scrambles over an arbor at a walkway that leads
from the rose garden to the dining terrace where white hydrangeas furnish accents
and a moss-laden hawthorn tree commands attention.

Three circular beds with boxwood globes and peacock topiaries perched on
cylinder plinths provide formality in the cottage garden. A spring display features
roses, peonies, delphiniums, and foxgloves, followed in the summer by mostly

Above: The entrance to the
house is set between projecting
wings.

Opposite: Garden rooms,
seen from the house, are
separated by yew hedges and
filled with boxwood frames
and topiaries; white Iceberg
floribunda roses stand out
against the green.

white flowers such as native Culver's root and double oriental lilies, another favorite of Caryn's. This almost maze-like bed arrangement beckons the visitor to travel all the bluestone paths.

When the Harrises purchased their property, there was a pool to the south. Stick suggested removing it to create woodland paths surrounding a large lawn. Today, an emerald greensward is bounded by gravel paths through evergreens that ensure privacy in the winter months. Pachysandra, hellebores, and ferns give different colors and textures to the woodland floor. Mophead clusters of hydrangeas have been strategically placed to furnish contrast to the vibrant greens and to be seen while wandering the paths. Whether walking through woodlands, blooming parterres, or the rose garden, the Harris garden offers understated sophistication.

Right: In a nod to English-style gardens, the formal boxwood parterres brim with shrub roses in shades of pink, coral, and white. Crab apple (*Malus sargentii 'Tina'*) standards and conic shaped boxwoods provide winter interest.

Above: The arbor connect-
ing the rose garden with the
dining terrace.

Above, right: Boxwood peacock topiaries complement
roses, peonies, foxgloves,
delphiniums, and catmint in
the perennial garden.

Overleaf: The motor court
features an ensemble of boxwood bushes tightly pruned
into ribbons and globes.

GARDEN HYBRID

HIGHLAND PARK

Chicago architect Arthur Heun designed this elegant Georgian revival house in 1930. There was no garden to speak of when, more than twenty years ago, the owners engaged landscape architect Scott Byron. "We asked Scott to 'clean up' the property," says the wife, while she mused about what type of garden would work best for the site and for the family. What she wanted was "a 'hybrid'—a blend of the formality of a French garden and the color and looseness of an English garden."

With a blank canvas, Byron's first task was to create an entryway garden to complement the handsome facade of the house. A gravel motor court, delineated by crab apple trees, and tiers of boxwood domes, pyramids, and hedges in geometric patterns, provides a verdant stage setting for arriving guests. An iron gate was installed to the south, where it creates a gracious entry to the garden and serves as an inviting focal point throughout the year.

A pool house and terrace rise gracefully to a commanding position via a flagstone retaining wall. Boxwood squares planted with New Guinea impatiens in a cross pattern surround Bradford pear trees. Standards of carefully trained lilacs stand near a mirrored glass sculpture by Jean-Michel Othoniel. Overlooking the pool house greensward is a commanding old gnarled hawthorn tree, which becomes a living sculpture to balance the modern glass beads on the upper terrace.

Above: An iron gate opens into a side garden filled with Bradford pear trees.

Opposite: Boston ivy—clad walls and layers of boxwood rectangles, filled with sculpted box globes, meld traditional plantings with contemporary design.

Distinct spaces for entertaining and family activities sit on different levels, each with a unique view. Planters overflowing with colorful perennial and seasonal plantings add a striking contrast to the structured verdant vistas.

The formal garden is the main attraction to the east. A classic concave stone wall, adorned with climbing roses and topped with four Regency-style urns, faces descending, semicircular grass and stone steps, and lends a decidedly English look. The wife and a floral designer friend worked with Byron to select the right plants, heights and colors for the flower borders. The jointly agreed palette includes pink and white roses and peonies, while shades of lavender and purple are seen in hydrangeas, lilacs, and alliums.

The cross axis of the formal garden is seen from a patterned boxwood parterre. It features an urn cascading with annuals and terminates across the bordering lawn with a smaller boxwood parterre and matching stone urn. The intervening grass served as a theater stage for the children when they were young. Today, the lawn can accommodate a long country-style table where guests dine in the English-inspired countryside garden.

The bold design of tailored boxwood hedges, globes, and parterres, together with the softness of richly planted mixed borders, is a harmonious and sophisticated background for family pleasures.

Right: Windows and terraces offer views of borders filled with peonies, phlox, daisies, alliums, lilacs, and annuals.

Left: Alliums add spring color to the formal garden where climbing hydrangea hugs the edges of a decorated demilune stone wall.

Above: A graceful, ancient
hawthorn tree is artistically
braced for support.

Top: Jean-Michel Othoniel's mirrored glass sculpture contrasts with the lilac standards and the tightly clipped boxwood.

Above: Dappled sunlight falls on boxwood squares and cones that anchor Bradford pear trees on the pool terrace.

BEAUTY WITHOUT BOUNDARIES

WINNETKA

For more than forty years, Shirley Ryan has championed efforts to maximize the abilities of individuals, including serving for nine years on the National Council on Disability as well as co-founding with her husband, Pat, Pathways. org in 1985—an out-patient pediatric clinic on the North Shore dedicated to motor, sensory, and communication development. Shirley's passion is to "focus positively on fostering pediatric abilities and potential and remove barriers to pediatric development."

When Shirley and Pat Ryan acquired land in 1992 on the North Shore for the home and garden of their dreams, they had two goals. First, they wanted an eighteenth-century style French manor house with two bedrooms on the first floor. Second, they wanted a house and garden that would be fully accessible and could be enjoyed by persons of all abilities.

With these objectives, the Francophile couple engaged architect Thomas Beeby, who fully appreciated their perspective and priorities. Beeby and his partner Gary Ainge worked with Stanley Falconer of Colefax and Fowler to create an exquisite manor house. Deborah Nevins was the landscape designer.

Above: An opening in the yew hedge provides a glimpse of the oval fountain in the lawn. A white magnolia Merrill is in bloom in the distance.

Opposite: Spring introduces early tulips, narcissus, and Virginia bluebells (*Mentensia Virginica*) along the gravel paths in the tulip garden.

Shirley knew she wanted the garden designed on the principles of universal accessibility, with smooth, broad paths and no steps. She also wanted numerous benches and seats for comfortable viewing and durable and easy-to-read plant identification markers with common and botanical names.

Encouraged by Nevins to visit select gardens for ideas and inspiration, the couple set off to see Dumbarton Oaks in Washington, Hidcote and Sissinghurst in England, and Chateau de Courances in France. They were enraptured by the perspective of the symmetrical lawns and shrubbery at Courances, and Nevins used this inspiration for the property.

A broad terrace of Yorkstone pavers, whose tight joints provide firm traction for shoes and wheels, overlooks a sweeping lawn surrounded by clipped yew hedging. Commanding attention from the terrace is an elegant, simple oval French pool and fountain backed by an American beech tree. Each of the adjoining garden rooms is accessed from this tapis vert.

As a young girl, Shirley developed a love of tulips because each May her parents took the family on a pilgrimage to Holland, Michigan, for the Tulip Festival. In response, Nevins designed a spectacular tulip garden under an allée of honey locusts. Shirley says, "We started out with all the tulips blooming more or less at the same time. We wanted the show to last longer, so we now have early, mid- and late-blooming tulips to celebrate Pat's May birthday all month long."

Today, the garden contains large drifts of tulips—hybrid and species, feathered and flamed, double and single bloom, parrot and fringed—in a rainbow of colors. These icons of spring mingle with Virginia bluebells, hellebores, leucojums, narcissus, astilbes, and hostas in a dazzling display.

Adjacent to the allée are two smaller garden rooms. In the first, yew hedges enclose a limestone-edged reflecting pool. A secret cloister garden with a yew parterre is more formal, with peacocks perched atop rounded domes. A Tudor wooden pergola, partially covered with wisteria, provides a beautiful backdrop.

Shirley wanted young swimmers developing their abilities to have a view from the interior pool. Nevins's solution is an "amphitheater," a sunken semicircular terrace with boxwood hugging the slope. Boxwoods are clipped into soft cushions, and the hillside is punctuated with four white-flowering crab apple trees.

Above: Tulips, of various cultivars, colors, and heights, are the stars of spring under the honey locust allée.

Terra-cotta pots filled with peony-shaped Angelique tulips line the walkway.

Overleaf: The green amphitheater features cushion-shaped boxwoods anchored by four crab apples.

Throughout the garden, five-foot-wide walkways afford views of the house and garden. These decomposed granite paths, which have been mixed with a stabilizer to ensure a non-slip surface, can accommodate two people, regardless of gait, chair, or cane. One "path through the woods," lined with perennials, provides those in chairs a rare opportunity to smell and feel the coolness of woods. Another passageway leads to a dell that serves a dual purpose—water retention and a home for dramatic water-loving plants.

The Ryans and Deborah Nevins have masterfully created a garden for people of all abilities. Their name for the garden, "Beauty Without Boundaries," is a perfect description of this unique place.

Opposite: Sweet alyssum and lady's mantle fill the crevices between stone steps.

Above: A granite path meanders through the dell, which features queen of the prairie (*Filipendula rubra*), ostrich ferns, iris, purple loosestrife (*Lythrum salicaria*), and giant butterbur (*Petasites japonicus*).

Above: Spouting frogs
perched on lily pads and the
edge of the reflecting pool are
whimsically named for mem-
bers of the Ryan family; blue
Cape plumbago cascades from
corner pots.

Top: The cloister garden features climbing wisteria on the Tudor-style pergola and boxwood parterres with topiary peacocks sculpted from yews.

Above: Towering hornbeam and yew hedges conceal the motor court from the garden.

BYRON GARDEN

HIGHLAND PARK

When landscape architect Scott Byron and his
wife, Maureen, purchased their house in the early
1990s, Scott saw great potential for the landscape.
However, with young children and a growing
business designing gardens for others, he did not
focus on creating their personal garden until a
decade later. At that time, Scott's quandary was,
"How do I create a garden when the house sits in
the middle of an acre site like a castle with a moat
around it?"

His answer was a classically inspired garden
with a robust framework of geometric lines and
sculptural elements surrounding "Maureen's
porch," a generous, screened space for dining,
entertaining, and enjoying the view. An admirer
of the famed landscape architect Thomas Church,
Byron created axial and cross-axial views by
producing garden rooms on three sides of the
porch. In effect, the porch became a courtyard
surrounded by garden rooms.

Seen from the entrance to the porch, the garden
allée becomes an extension of the house. The allée
has classic features—pleached Armstrong maples
with silver-gray bark planted in square boxwood hedges. Low lattice walls act
both as background for the allée and, at the same time, demarcate small areas for
perennial beds on the opposite side. A stone hardscape, urns planted with ferns,
and an antique bench that serves as a focal point in front of an arborvitae hedge
add to the formality.

Above: The formal garden
has axial and cross-axial
views created by extensive
box hedging.

Opposite: An antique bench
nestles into a boxwood frame
flanked by the pleached
Armstrong maple allée.

A bluestone terrace that abuts the porch and dining room features tree lilacs. The
main focus is an Aqualens sphere fountain designed by Allison Armour. This
contemporary mark blends perfectly into the more traditional atmosphere.
Throughout the garden, tailored boxwood squares and rectangles have been
planted with annuals, roses, or euonymus. Various plant textures and shapes, all
in shades of green, give a unified and elegant feel to the garden.

The north–south long axis runs from the upper garden to the south lawn with
drifts of Annabelle hydrangeas and white begonias on either side. A grouping of
three antique Cotswold stone spheres of varying sizes on the greensward lends a

striking element. Maureen Byron, who formerly had
an antique garden ornament business, contributed this
feature as well as other troughs, pots, and containers
that overflow with annuals and succulents.

Scott Byron's personal garden demonstrates his skill
at manipulating spaces regardless of size. With robust
structural design and repetition, he has created a sense
of an increased landscape and a melodious rhythm
surrounding his "castle."

Opposite: Fern-laden urns
provide textural contrast and
vertical interest.

Above: Surrounded by tree
lilacs, Allison Armour's contemporary Aqualens fountain
is the focal point on the bluestone terrace.

Top: Annabelle hydrangeas at dusk.

Above: The woodland setting includes drifts of begonias, pachysandra, hydrangeas, and variegated hostas.

Opposite: Antique Cotswold stone spheres punctuate the lawn.

CLINOLA

LAKE FOREST

Howard Van Doren Shaw designed this Georgian revival country house for his friend and Yale classmate Thomas E. Donnelley in 1911. The extensive property included a formal Italianate garden room created in 1927 by landscape architect Ferruccio Vitale, as well as perennial borders, a wildflower walk, and cutting and vegetable gardens. The property remained in the Donnelley family until 2009, when Stephanie and John Harris became the stewards.

Stephanie's parents live nearby, and when young she often walked past the house and along the back of the property while hiking in the adjoining Lake Forest Open Lands prairie. When the property came on the market, the couple saw an extraordinary opportunity to restore and enhance the house and gardens.

Above: The house seen from a grove of ostrich fern and pachysandra.

Opposite: Rose spirea line a path to a Chippendale-style gate set in the hornbeam hedge surrounding the large potager garden.

"Doing right by the house and landscape" is the motto for all their restoration and enhancement efforts. To direct garden activities, they chose Charles Stick, a Virginia-based landscape architect who had worked with their parents and was already a friend of both families.

The footprint of the early twentieth-century gardens guided Stick's designs, which scrupulously respect the past. Vitale's fanciful formal garden was refurbished, based on copies of his drawings passed on from the previous owner and old photographs, with new lattice paneling, boxwood hedges, and compatible plantings. The descending lawn, with original lead urns on corner plinths, leads to a replica of the Roman sculpture *Diana de Versailles*, which stands in a trellis alcove behind a small pool.

On the generous terrace that wraps around the west side of the house, Stick has imaginatively installed a large crisply cut boxwood parterre in the bluestone paving. Stephanie says, "I like greenery in the middle of the terrace. The less hardscape, the better." Looking west from the French doors in the library, the formality of the parterre diminishes as the sweeping lawn with its flower borders on one side transitions into the prairie, a magnificent view throughout the day but especially at sunset.

To the north of the lawn, tall hornbeam hedges, pierced with white Chippendale-style gate openings, enclose an exquisite "vegetable garden" as Stephanie calls her love. The walled garden roughly follows the same footprint as the original, but Stick divided the space into two areas—a parterre garden and a pure vegetable garden. Peonies form a low hedge against two walls of the parterre garden. Boxwood-edged quadrant beds, anchored with apple trees, some old, some new, gracefully display perennials and roses that spill over their boundaries. A circle of white roses frames a weathered stone wellhead.

In late summer, the vegetable section explodes with heirloom tomatoes, squash, Brussels sprouts, herbs, and rows of raspberries for the children to pick, and of course, pumpkins. The vista from the west garden gates onto the adjoining prairie, with its ever-changing sea of blazing star, goldenrod, and grasses, is breathtaking.

A low native fieldstone wall marks the border between the property and the Open Lands prairie beyond. From this vantage point, the long-mixed border backed by the hornbeam hedge comes into closer view. "As the seasons progress," Stephanie says, "I sometimes go plant shopping to fill in areas that might need more punch." Her handiwork has produced an intensely planted border where phlox, daisies and bee balm mingle with coneflowers, yarrow, Culver's root, irises, and lilies.

Whether it's the mixed border, the "vegetable garden," the Vitale garden, parterre west terrace, or other garden areas surrounding Clinola, the Harrises and Charles Stick have achieved their objective of "doing right by the house and landscape."

Right: Designed by Ferruccio Vitale in 1927, the formal garden is bounded by arts-and-crafts lattice paneling. The descending lawn, surrounded by perennial borders, terminates with a small pool and a replica of *Diana de Versailles* in the trellis alcove.

Right: A hornbeam hedge
encloses a formal garden
that features four large boxwood parterres with old
apple trees. Iceberg floribunda roses and perenni-
als, including Shasta daisies,
Culver's root, phlox, astilbes,
and cranesbill geranium,
fill the spaces. An antique
wellhead and herb parterres
complete the design.

Above: A neatly clipped hornbeam hedge separates the flower garden from the vegetables in the walled garden.

Above, right: Ripening apples and Brussels sprouts signal harvest time is near. Beyond the garden gate is the golden glow of prairie sunflowers.

Overleaf: An intricate box-wood parterre provides greenery on the rear blue-stone terrace, which opens onto a greensward and prairie beyond. Mixed borders offer seasonal color alongside the walled garden to the right and at the fieldstone wall that marks the border between the lawn and the prairie.

EDGECLIFF

WINNETKA

Edgecliff, as its name suggests, is sited on the cliffs above Lake Michigan. The French manor house inspired by eighteenth-century Normandy estates was designed by Beaux-Arts architect Samuel Marx and completed in 1930. The extensive landscape was designed by Katherine Brewster, one of the founders of the Lake Forest Garden Club and the Garden Club of America.

Donna and Terry McKay purchased the property in 1995 and set about restoring both the house and gardens. In 2014 landscape architect Craig Bergmann was commissioned to reimagine the grounds within the historical Brewster outline and hardscape established earlier. The couple wanted more color and diverse plantings for summer activities while retaining unobstructed views of Lake Michigan.

Above: Autumn brings brilliant orange hues to the maple allée extending from the twin gatehouses to the motor court.

Opposite: Lead containers filled with pale and deep pink geraniums, purple petunias, and coleus flank the front door.

Overleaf: The walled garden displays a limestone-edged fountain and lawn panel surrounded by mixed borders and antique urns spilling with fuschia.

The house is approached by an arching maple allée that terminates with lead eagles welcoming visitors to the gravel motor court. The elegant but straightforward French architecture, covered with climbing euonymus, is a dramatic background for lead planters overflowing with colorful seasonal plantings. A wooden Chippendale-style gate opens from the courtyard into the large, formal walled garden.

Standing tall on plinths, glazed terra-cotta figures of the Four Seasons overlook a lush border of dahlias, astilbes, asters, hydrangeas, and other perennials. Bergmann designed an art deco–inspired fountain, with a zinc bowl cascading into a limestone capped basin, for the center of the enclosed lawn. An arborvitae hedge acts as the southern wall with an obelisk centered among a shrub border of false spiraea, dogwood, and tree lilacs.

The doorway on the west wall, with climbing hydrangea draped on a graceful wood canopy, is the gateway to a large woodland area where heritage white oak trees provide a high canopy. Serpentine gravel paths wander among beds of hostas, hydrangeas, grasses, Joe Pye weed, and goldenrod. Bottlebrush and *Heptacodium*, or Seven Sons Tree, furnish a green understory.

Leading from the walled garden to the lakeside lawn is an intimate and charming parterre with a stone sundial surrounded by gray and purple plantings. Craig

has created a new take on a parterre garden by using perennials, such as lamb's ears and silvery Powis Castle, as boxwood substitutes.

Sitting areas overlooking the expansive greensward and lake allow the McKay family to enjoy the ever-changing moods of Lake Michigan. A bramble of little bluestem and coneflowers at the lawn's edge celebrates the rising sun horizon.

Approached by descending stairs crowned by large Swedish cast-iron urns, the east terrace is a beautiful combination of vibrant plantings and elegant architecture. Double-tiered mixed borders, with the lower bed planted at the same level as the pool, give swimmers ground-level views of iris, phlox, summer allium, coneflowers, dahlias, and other perennials.

When Terry McKay asked Bergmann to repurpose the leftover clay roof tiles, he suggested a pergola with columns similar to what Christopher Lloyd created for a loggia at Great Dixter. This wisteria-covered space is used frequently by the family for dining and conversation while they watch the grandchildren "swim among the flowers." Completing the magnificent setting is a convex grassed belvedere ringed with periwinkle hydrangeas looking out to the lake.

Right: In summer, the formal mixed border brims with astilbes, balloon flowers, dahlias, and panicle hydrangea (*H. paniculata 'Tardiva'*).

Opposite: A vigorous trumpet vine and pear espalier encircles a poolhouse window. The two-tiered perennial border features betony, coneflower, phlox, summer allium, iris and plumbago.

Top: A pergola, inspired by the Great Dixter garden in Sussex, England, overlooks the pool terrace and a double border of cool-colored perennials.

Above: The grass belvedere, ringed with a hedge of periwinkle hydrangeas (*H. macrophylla 'Twist-n-Shout'*), offers a view of Lake Michigan.

CROWE GARDEN

LAKE FOREST

This elegant Georgian revival house, designed by Howard Van Doren Shaw and completed in 1907, has a distinguished past for both its architecture and the surrounding gardens. The first owners commissioned Charles A. Platt and Rose Standish Nichols, both of the Cornish Colony in New Hampshire, to design the overall estate and planting. When Peggy Crowe and her late husband, Jack, purchased the property in 1990, little of the Platt and Nichols work remained. As a Renaissance couple with a focus on decorative arts and gardens, the Crowes set out to restore and enhance the house and grounds.

On a tour of the RHS Chelsea Flower Show in London, a fellow Lake Forest gardener advised them to ask English garden designer Rosemary Verey to plan the garden. Verey agreed to visit and give her ideas for an English-style garden. Not familiar with what would grow best in the Midwest, she collaborated with local landscape architect Craig Bergmann on plant selection.

Above and opposite: A sculpture by John Kearney terminates the allée of scaling-bark plane trees. Adjoining the allée, wide grass steps descend from the east terrace to a greensward.

Verey suggested creating adjoining garden rooms, which can be enjoyed from the raised terrace and from inside the house. A brick wall encloses one side of the garden rooms while impressive yew hedges bolster the opposite side. A bubbling fountain surrounded by formal, low-clipped boxwood is the centerpiece of the lilac room. Beyond, a comfortable bench awaits visitors where they can take in the garden's stunning sightlines. An adjacent room with four quadrants of soft-colored perennials burst forth in early summer, including alliums and foxgloves mixed with lady's mantle and pink-flowered astilbe, along with white butterfly bush and blue ageratum later in the season. Adjoining the Verey-designed garden rooms, Bergmann created a rectangular space with a colonial-style festoon chain of climbing pink roses underplanted with chartreuse-flowered lady's mantle and blue-violet perennial geraniums.

The Crowes, inveterate travelers, visited gardens wherever they went and brought back dreams for their garden. Jack designed the allée of mottled-bark plane trees, which provides a spectacular view from the doorway in the east wall. John Kearney's horse sculpture presides over the allée, while along the edges of the gravel path are many terra-cotta pots filled with boxwood globes. From the allée, wide grass steps

created by the couple come into view. Peggy Crowe says, "we decided to add grace and open up the front lawn with steps as the old terrace balustrade was deteriorating." Now graceful steps lead from the east terrace to a park-like lawn.

On a tour with the Garden Conservancy Society of Fellows to Newport, the Crowes saw a replica of the Derby Summer House designed in 1793 by Massachusetts architect Samuel McIntire. Jack fell in love with this folly and was determined to replicate it. Today, the two-story Federal-style garden house serves as a pool house as well as a backdrop for two herb-filled parterres.

This idyllic property is enhanced by the cohesion and strong structure of carefully pruned hedges and trees. Boxwood hedges, with colonial-style gate openings, border the gravel entrance drive while pleached hornbeam standards in popsicle and cone shapes surround the pool terrace. All the neatly trimmed shrubs and trees seem to be standing at attention as this jubilant garden parade passes by.

Above: The gravel drive winds past the pool terrace, where pleached hornbeam standards screen the view of the replica of the Derby Summer House.

Above: Rosemary Verey designed the lilac room, with its bubbling round fountain, boxwood, hydrangeas, and lilacs. The statue by Simon Verity is called "Rosie" in her honor.

Above: The quadrant garden room, designed by Verey, erupts with phlox, roses, salvia, lilies, ageratum, and white butterfly bush (*Buddleia davidii 'White Profusion'*) during the summer. In spring (opposite, top) iris, foxgloves, alliums, peonies, and lady's mantle fill the beds. A growing rose garland (opposite, below) is suspended from iron chains between colonial posts.

HALCYON LODGE

LAKE FOREST

The Colvin sisters were the original owners of Halcyon Lodge, which was designed by Howard Van Doren Shaw in 1905. When the current owner and her late husband purchased the property in 1983, the only garden "bones" on the site were parterre outlines in the "side garden," as the wife calls the space, and an axial formal garden with a glorious old fountain anchoring the long vista from the house. The wife—the gardener in the family and an accomplished artist—set about the task of reinvigorating the garden and adding new features, always mindful of the original spirit and overall layout.

The owner's design and color sense can be seen in her changes and additions to the garden over the years. The parterre garden originally consisted of four large quadrants surrounding a fountain and fishpond. "There was way too much garden in each bed, so I reduced the size of each quadrant by several feet to provide for larger grass pathways," she explains. She created more formality by planting low boxwood hedges around each bed, punctuated by corner globes. The original fountain is no longer present, but four limestone fruit baskets continue to grace the large pond.

The side garden is an enchanting space from spring to fall with continually changing colors. In spring, tulips emerge in vibrant colors accented with dainty white-flowered spring leucojums. Towering pink- and white-flowering crab apple trees surround the area. In summer pink, white, and blue, with touches of yellow, take over as peonies, daisies, phlox, catmint, and meadow rue bloom profusely. Rose beds, along with a pergola covered with porcelain berry, and a seating crescent complement the pool house.

Beside the house, within climbing hydrangea-covered brick walls, is a small kitchen garden designed by landscape architect Doug Hoerr. Four different types of heirloom apple trees anchor the space with an adjacent herb and container garden where sweet peas and roses scamper across trellis-covered walls in summer. Further along, Hoerr designed an intimate enclosed secret garden where seating encourages the visitor to enjoy the beauty of the purple weeping beech. An opening in the tall arborvitae hedge, which is on direct axis to the centennial fountain beyond, beckons visitors into the formal courtyard garden.

Above: A courtyard garden framed with box and white perennial borders is set between the wings of the house.

Opposite: In late summer, boxwood parterres in the side garden are filled with phlox, spider flowers (*Cleome*), catmint, coneflowers, and prairie sunflowers.

In 2003 architect Thomas Beeby designed two one-story wings entirely in keeping with the Shaw design. These additions allowed for the creation of an elegant terrace and grassed courtyard with double mixed borders focused on the original stone fountain and its moss-covered shell details. Edged in boxwood, the "white" borders—with mock orange shrubs and hydrangeas, white-flowered perennials and annuals—are highlighted by Regency-style urns with lattice backgrounds covered in white clematis.

The house is surrounded on the south side by a ravine, which features some naturalistic plantings designed by O. C. Simonds, landscape "gardener," as he liked to be called, and Prairie School founder.

Right: Matching "white" borders in the courtyard garden include mock orange shrubs, hydrangeas, peonies, phlox, nicotiana, and snapdragons. Lead urns sit in lattice-backed alcoves covered with white clematis.

Right: Spring arrives in the side garden with blooms from pink crab apples and a rainbow of tulip cultivars and leucojum in the parterres.

Overleaf: The side gaden blooms profusely by September with four quadrants of phlox, cleome, zinnias, prairie sunflowers, catmint, and daisies.

CAMP ROSEMARY

LAKE FOREST

The name "Camp Rosemary" comes from the daily ritual when construction crew working on the restoration of this property camped out on the lawn for lunch. This name, given by the fun-loving and hospitable owner, in no way describes her creation of one of the most exquisite English-style gardens in America.

The house is approached from a linden allée opening onto a square motor court bordered on either side by heritage oaks and bentgrass lawns mowed in precise stripes. Landscape gardener Rose Standish Nichols established the broad greensward and the garden rooms enclosed by yew hedges that hug the ivy-clad house designed by Benjamin Marshall in 1904.

Some of the bones of the Nichols garden rooms survive today, but the owner has used her innate design and horticultural expertise to fill them with exuberance and delight. The dominant colors throughout the gardens are shades of purple, blue, and pink—the gardener's favorites. This palette is displayed in the west terrace parterre garden with perennials and annuals surrounded by boxwood hedges and yew walls and highlighted with urns spilling with lavender. Adjacent is an enchanting thyme garden, which also can be enjoyed from the living room.

More extensive borders of color appear in the "pergola garden," the first mixed border garden created by the owner. A tall undulating hedge, trimmed in honor of a visit by Piet Oudolf, provides a dramatic backdrop. The pergola, covered with lush clematis and roses, affords a shaded spot from which to view borders of salvias, phlox, dahlias, artemisia, and other perennials mingling with cosmos and cleome, all flourishing around a circular stone fountain.

Two tall Chinese female figures guard the chapel-like white garden, inspired by Nichols. Black-bottomed rectangular pools at either end reflect the sky, pine trees, and white blossoms of dogwoods, whitebuds, and hydrangeas. Variegated brunnera and towering white bugbane create an elegant and ethereal feel to this intimate space, the site of both weddings and baptisms.

Further on, wide grass steps, inspired by those at Dumbarton Oaks, descend into the magnificent walled garden. Many noted landscape designers have contributed to this expansive garden, including Craig Bergmann, Frank Mariani, Clifford

Above: The living room bay overlooks a carpet of violet, purple, and white sweet alyssum; urns and pots of blue scaevola and lavender provide accents.

Opposite: From the thyme garden, straight bent lawn stripes extend to a generous curve of pink roses and an antique urn overflowing with pink geraniums and white guara.

Miller, Deborah Nevins, and Rosemary Verey. Nevins suggested the large copper beech hedge that curves around the ancient ash tree centerpiece. Brick walls anchor displays of perennials and annuals, some rarely seen, and supplemented by shrubs and roses. In this space, the garden composer has added occasional splashes of yellow and orange to her garden palette. The backdrop is a raised platform, again reached by broad grass steps, with an elegant William and Mary–style pool pavilion designed by architect Thomas Beeby and his wife, Kirsten. Luxuriant clematis scampering over brick walls in the double-bordered rose garden greets the visitor. All of this beauty is best seen from the second-floor window of the pool pavilion, the owner's favorite spot.

On either side of the pavilion are boxwood knot gardens in different designs and a linden allée interspersed with terra-cotta pots sporting boxwood globes. Antique pots, lead and stone urns, along with classical statuary, play supporting roles throughout the gardens. These containers are placed in strategic positions, bursting forth each year with striking combinations of perennials and annuals. Plants occupy every niche of this property—in borders, in pots, on walls, in cracks—and extend to the sky.

Completing the property is a wooded ravine walk with native shrubs, including witch hazel, viburnum, and redbud complementing a native carpet of wild geranium, trillium, Virginia bluebell, May apple, and Jack-in-the-pulpit. An adjoining circular grass labyrinth has been allowed to grow taller and provides a touch of whimsy.

The garden-conductor of Camp Rosemary has produced a magical garden composition that demonstrates the highest quality of horticulture and artful design. Her ideas and vision for colors, plant combinations, structure and whimsical touches are the keys to this jewel.

Above: The owner's first mixed border was developed in the pergola garden with the ornamental Bradford pear hedge as a backdrop.

Her favorite colors—pink, fuchsia, lavender, and blue—can be seen in veronica, betony, delphinium, and cosmos. Artemisia (*A. ludoviciana*

'*Silver King*') is peppered throughout.

Overleaf: The ivy-clad pool pavilion overlooks the walled garden with its mixed borders, rose beds, and containers. The linden allée is adjacent.

Above: In the walled garden,
several varieties of clematis
scramble over brick walls
that define sweeping bor-
ders filled with shrub roses,
perennials, and annuals.

Top: The rose garden is a symphony of pink and purple with blush pink roses hugging brick walls covered with pink, blue, and purple clematis; lily of the Nile (*Agapanthus*) with its lavender-blue flowers is often featured in containers throughout the garden rooms.

Above: Broad grass steps, modelled after those at Dumbarton Oaks, create an impressive entrance to the walled garden.

Right: The white garden is an intimate alcove surrounded by hydrangeas, bugbane, variegated dogwood, flowering dogwood, and perennials.

Above: A metal apple tree sculpture is the focal point in this boxwood parterre adjoining the pavilion.

Above, right: A gravel terrace, randomly placed boxwood-filled terra-cotta pots, and bistro chairs create a French atmosphere in the pleached linden allée.

Overleaf: A combination of blue and lavender perennials and annuals, with white and lavender roses on the outer edges, fills the parterre garden.

CONTEMPORARY GARDENS

BLUHM GARDEN

WINNETKA

A sleek contemporary house tucked into a slope on the Winnetka shoreline is the setting for this garden. The building, designed by modernist architect Peter Gluck a decade ago for Amy and Andy Bluhm, minimizes its impact on the three-acre property while taking advantage of the majesty of Lake Michigan. The glass facade rises two stories at the entrance, but, on the shore side, the four-story glass and steel structure unfolds as a series of planes down a forty-two-foot bluff, each with commanding lake views.

Amy Bluhm, "the garden director" in the family, wanted a landscape that "felt natural for the location of the house and always had something in the wings" with a succession of plants emerging. The Bluhms commissioned landscape architect Doug Hoerr because they admired his artistic blend of naturalistic and contemporary landscapes. The landscape design juxtaposes two different environments—a woodland meadow at the front of the house and in the rear geometric plantings and strategically placed trees through which striking views of the lake emerge.

Old weathered reclaimed-wood fencing surrounds the property. Both sides of the entry are planted with tulips, hellebores, and hostas in the spring and give way to giant butterbur in the summer.

Although Amy wanted a drive straight to the house, Hoerr convinced her that a winding approach would highlight the landscape. The entrance road now curves gently through swamp white oak, maples, and aspens. Mature trees and shrubs provide a sense of enclosure and age. In spring, the area is ablaze with thousands of snowdrops, tulips, alliums, grape hyacinths, leucojums, and narcissus.

In summer, a large lawn provides an area for family activities. Bold drifts of beardtongues, asters, and dahlias socializing with astilbe, ferns, and daisies, along with massed plantings of grasses, give the landscape surprises at each bend in the road. For visitor parking, Hoerr created an area with islands of small trees and shrubs underplanted with perennials and roses.

Above: Alongside a stone staircase, a panel of evergreen wintercreeper (*Euonymous fortunei 'Coloatus'*) flows from one terrace to another.

Opposite: Early summer brings blue spires of baptisia, a native prairie plant, to the hillside overlooking Lake Michigan.

Near the house, the design changes to a more contemporary concept. Whether entering the house or descending a grassy slope, the spectacular vista and beauty of Lake Michigan and its changing moods take center stage. With this backdrop of sparkling blue water, Hoerr created layers of green, using different textures, colors, and compositions spilling from the top of the bluff down to the sandy shore. He enhanced the angular architectural elements with flowing landforms and vegetation. The hillside has hardy rugosa roses tucked among bayberry, dune grass, Sargent juniper, and *Verbena bonariensis*.

Terraces on different levels offer options for dining, entertainment, and sports activities. Descending from an upper level to the pool is a wide grass slope with adjacent triangles and rectangles of euonymous. The landscaping on these two levels, which also act as rooftop gardens, is architectural and geometric in style with impressive beds of single plant cultivars. Beyond the upper terraces, shrubs, and grasses, the descending bluff pathway ends at a sandy beach planted with dune grass. A boathouse is built into the bluff, allowing vistas from the terraces of a verdant shoreline without interruption.

Right: The entrance drive meanders through a woodland of mature native trees. White astilbe and a raised bed of lilac alliums provide pops of color.

Above: Spring-blooming tulips, hellebores, and May apples at the drive entrance; in the woodland tulips create a carpet of color.

Opposite: Across the lawn, redbud trees bloom in late spring, attracting scores of pollinators.

Overleaf: Views of Lake Michigan unfold on the descent from one terrace level to another.

Above: Drifts of lady's mantle
(*Alchemilla mollis*), orna-
mental allium, and betony
(*Stachys officinalis 'Hummelo'*)

carpet the woodland drive;
lilac-colored Chinese astilbe
thrives under the aspen trees.

CRAB TREE FARM SUMMER HOUSE

LAKE BLUFF

In 2008 Neville Bryan and her late husband, John, decided to build the Summer House for their children and grandchildren. As a foil to the traditional architecture of the main house, Chicago architect John Vinci designed a two-story glass-and-stucco building with an asymmetrically placed viewing tower overlooking farmland and the historic dairy complex.

Belgian landscape architect Peter Wirtz, son of the legendary Jacques Wirtz, designed a contemporary setting. At the entrance, tailored hornbeam hedges enclose mounded yews under a canopy of walnut trees. Close to the house on the opposite side, tightly spaced and formally clipped hornbeam hedging encloses the pool and creates a maze-like effect that gracefully opens onto the adjoining pasture. Near the pool house is a remarkable pergola with mottled bark plane tree trunks and a pollarded canopy giving rhythm and structure. At the closed end sits a prototype plate for *Cloud Gate* (colloquially known as "The Bean") by Anish Kapoor. John Bryan led the successful private sector fundraising efforts for Chicago's Millennium Park, where the finished sculpture is installed.

Three reflecting canals, staggered and placed parallel to each other, create interest in the middle ground between the garden terrace and the alfalfa fields. To counterbalance this elegant simplicity, Wirtz created a swelling grass mound, much like an Indian mound, that adds motion to the landscape, screens the view from the road and provides a belvedere-like viewing podium of the canals and fields. A nearby raised grid platform of thirty white-flowering crab apple trees provides another perspective of this dynamic landscape.

Above: Yews shaped into low mounds form the understory beneath black walnut trees.

Opposite: Asymmetrical hornbeam hedges provide dramatic linkage with the adjacent pastures.

Overleaf: Canals between the garden terrace and the alfalfa fields reflect the house and ever-changing sky and cloudscapes.

Above: White-flowered
Donald Wyman crab apples
are planted on a grid.

Top: A giant lawn mound, reminiscent of Indian mounds, acts as a belvedere for viewing the contemporary landscape.

Above: Meticulously clipped hedges impose a disciplined geometry on the landscape close to the house, contrasting with the open fields beyond.

Overleaf: Plane tree branches meet to create a "living" pergola, which is reflected by the mirrored surface of a prototype piece of Anish Kapoor's monumental sculpture *Cloud Gate*.

GARDEN OF CURVES

WINNETKA

The owners of this two-acre property lived in a Tudor-style stucco and timber house for almost forty years before they decided to build a contemporary house in its place. For this project, they chose architect Larry Booth, who designed an elegant two-story stucco pavilion that rises from the earth with large floor-to-ceiling windows trimmed with zinc. To enhance the wooded and rural atmosphere of the site, the couple selected landscape architect Doug Hoerr, who often works with Booth. Hoerr has created a contemporary design of naturalistic plantings that complements the house.

The wife, an amateur landscape photographer, describes her style as "Zen-like—clean, beautiful lines that are comfortable." Although she did not suggest changes to the plans, the gardens Hoerr designed reflect her preferences.

Above and opposite: Irregular herringbone stone walls contain the swale of lawn, providing beds for quaking aspens and Indian hyacinth (*Camassia quamash*) and creating raised herbaceous borders boasting astilbe, *Verbena bonariensis*, blue ageratum, daisies, and lilies.

This section of Winnetka was once low-lying marshland. Hoerr used the topography to his advantage by designing a curving lawn, which makes a strong design statement and creatively fulfills the stormwater code requirements. Serpentine stone walls, in an irregular herringbone pattern, rim adjacent island mounds, creating a fluid motion that sweeps the eye through the site and makes it feel larger than it is. Shimmering aspens, conifers, and flowering crab apple trees provide a soft canopy on these raised islands for a luxuriantly planted tapestry of spreading juniper, lady's mantle, Russian sage, astilbe, other perennials, and spring-blooming bulbs.

This is a garden for wandering and exploring. Winding pathways of Wisconsin stone and grass thread their way past hydrangea and bottlebrush, allowing for unfolding vistas both near and far. There is an urge to stop, look around, and see what is blooming or about to come into bud. Adding to the enjoyment is the host of wildlife that brings the garden alive with sound. The beauty of the shapes, colors, and textures of flowers and shrubs, along with the bird songs, is captivating.

Right: Ornamental allium brightens the foreground while quaking aspen, ginkgo, and white pine trees provide vertical structure.

Closer to the house are touches of an Asian aesthetic. In the entry courtyard, a trio of rough-cut cyclopean stone slabs is positioned in front of rhododendron, rodgersia, and boxwood. Pachysandra and hardy geranium soften the edges of the warm-colored dry ashlar pavers. Off the living area is a similar stone terrace planted with Siberian iris, barberry, and geranium. The views of the garden from inside become art walls within the house.

The long driveway, a portion of which is the only straight line in the garden, connects the property with two neighboring streets. Hoerr designed various verdant vignettes along the gravel and grass drive that are backed by sophisticated steel fencing and, again, beautifully crafted herringbone stone walls. The groupings of shrubbery and trees, all partnered with grasses and perennials, provide a natural border for the property and result in a very private garden.

Opposite: Complementing the contemporary style of the house is an Asian-influenced entrance garden. Giant wedges of stone are surrounded by rhododendrum, rodgersia, pachysandra, and ferns in different shades of green.

Above: A path winds through the woodland with carpets of lady's mantle and ornamental allium.

Above: In early June, blue
stars (*Amsonia*) and salvia
provide color in the raised
beds.

Top: Stone steps lead to a woodland filled with lady's mantle and grasses, pink astilbe, and bottlebrush buckeye in the distance.

Above: Annabelle hydrangeas and ornamental alliums mark the entrance.

COUNTRY GARDENS

METTAWA MANOR

METTAWA

What type of garden do you get when you combine the talents of one of the most civic-minded women in Chicago with a nationally known broadcaster and documentary producer? The answer is a melodious garden symphony. This is what Donna LaPietra and Bill Kurtis have produced at Mettawa Manor.

The couple purchased the 1927 Tudor revival manor house and nine acres in 1990 and became the property's second owner. Having lived in Chicago, the couple had little experience with country-style living and even less with restoring gardens or creating new ones.

Donna La Pietra hired landscape architect Craig Bergmann to tackle the restoration of the formal sunken walled garden, which extends from the rear terrace. Today, this centerpiece is an enclosed English-style garden with two forty-foot herbaceous borders, backed by juniper hedges, that flank a sunken lawn. At the end of the lawn is a boxwood parterre surrounding a Venetian marble wellhead. Overflowing perennial beds on either side of double wrought-iron gates bring spring and summer color to this part of the garden.

Above: Silver globes of different sizes in the Reflection Garden.

Opposite: A lilac standard highlights one of the mixed borders in the walled garden.

A smaller gate to the east opens onto the ever-changing meadow. Bergmann suggested the plant procession that begins in spring with hundreds of colonizing bulbs—narcissus, followed by fritillaria and camassia. In late summer, after the meadow is mowed, Queen Anne's lace emerges. An espaliered apple tree cordon fence separates the meadow from the nearby cutting and vegetable garden. Here, iron arbors provide support for cherry tomatoes, beans, and other vegetables with beds abloom with zinnias, phlox, and daisies.

The couple is always creating new gardens or adding features to existing gardens. They are assisted by garden designer Kathleen Reynolds, who has worked with them for more than twenty years. A few years ago, they created a double linden allée in the foreground of their prairie. This allée has a captivating carpet of buttercups in the spring. Nearby is the Gold Garden filled with shrubs and perennials in all shades of yellow and orange.

Growing up in Kansas, Bill Kurtis was surrounded by tallgrass prairie. He says, "At evening time, with the sun setting over our prairie, the light is magical like *The Wizard of Oz*." Over time, the couple has purchased adjacent properties, and today Mettawa

Right: An English-style mixed border, including Joe Pye weed, betony, obedient plant (*Physotegia Virginia*), and spider plant, flanks the sunken lawn.

Manor encompasses sixty-five acres, of which about thirty are prairie. After removing acres of invasive shrubs, Kurtis has developed a magnificent natural prairie where deep-rooted native plants such as snakeroot, blazing star, goldenrod, and other forbs bloom with vigor in late July and early August. As he observes, "We have liberated these long-forgotten plants. We eagerly watch each spring to see what next species will emerge."

Overlooking the prairie is an Indian mound created from earth removed from excavations on the property. The mound has three levels, each providing the visitor with a different perspective of the prairie and the gardens.

Near the west side of the house is the Aquatheater Garden, a setting for music and theatrical performances on a grass island surrounded by water and tall juniper hedges. A recent addition on the east side is the Reflection Garden—silver and gold spheres lying on pine straw and cones in an old white pine grove.

As the couple has developed gardens and prairies over the last thirty years, they have been guided by the conservation maxim "listen to the land." When they first arrived at Mettawa, they watched the disappearance of honeybees, monarch butterflies, and some bird species. Today, luxuriant gardens and prairie plants attract bees and butterflies in search of nectar and birds fly and swoop in large numbers over the land.

Right: Fragrant butterfly bush, bee balm, and Russian sage offer a palette of soft colors in the forty-foot long double borders.

Above: The Aquatheater
offers a lawn platform, with an
evergreen background, as
a stage for performances.

Top: Chartreuse-leaved smokebush, yellow-flowered yarrow, and lupines are three of the colorful perennials and shrubs in the Golden Garden.

Above: A Venetian marble wellhead sets off the boxwood parterre and rose beds at the end of the sunken garden.

Top: Wide double rows of creeping buttercups (*Ranunculus repens*) create yellow carpets beneath the linden allée in early spring.

Above: Espaliered apple trees separate the vegetable garden from the meadow.

Above: Drifts of white- and yellow-cup narcissus fill the meadow in early spring followed by Indian hyacinth.

Overleaf: Three mounds, each with seating, provide views of the prairie with its glowing blazing star (*Liatris*) and other native plants.

BALUSEK GARDEN

WINNETKA

Ann and Brian Balusek's passion for gardening begin when they were children and worked in their parents' gardens. When they were first married and lived in downtown Chicago, they took classes in perennials, shrubs, and turf at the Chicago Botanic Garden and "learned to garden together."

The couple fell in love at first sight with their 1923 manor house designed by New York architect Alfred Hopkins. Hopkins, who specialized in country houses and gentleman's farms, had previously designed the Elawa Farm barn and stable buildings in Lake Forest. The mellow Cotswold-style house, with elegant stucco detailing, provided the perfect setting for them to demonstrate their gardening skills.

Above: The hornbeam bower shelters a vintage statue at the entry to the motor court.

Opposite: A faux-bois dovecote is tucked away in this shady nook with astilbes, hostas, ferns, and hydrangeas.

Soon after moving in 2010, the Baluseks contacted landscape architect Craig Bergmann, who had designed several garden spaces for the previous owners. He and the Baluseks collaborated on a series of "pocket gardens" around the house, much like its interior, which has many small rooms.

A well-weathered stone figure of an English country gentleman, surrounded by a hornbeam bower, greets visitors arriving at the motor court. Boxwood, climbing hydrangeas, and large pots with annuals encircle the cloistered entrance off the motor court. To the right of the doorway is the shade garden, a verdant combination of astilbes, hostas, ferns, and hydrangeas.

The shade garden inspired the Baluseks to transform a screened porch into "a glass room within a garden," giving them views of the garden year-round. Hidden in the shade garden, poised on a tree trunk, is an faux-bois dovecote, one of the many garden ornaments found in the garden. Over the years, the couple has collected statuary, finials, and containers on their travels. Strategically placed throughout the garden, these elements add interest and whimsy.

Beyond the shade garden is the terrace garden with its generous pergola entwined with an old trumpet vine and sweet autumn clematis. Flagstone steps, anchored by a pair of robust yew globes, lead to the upper stone and grass terrace with dining and sitting areas. Cascading borders explode with colorful plantings from spring to fall. Ann is a master at mixed plantings, placing peonies, roses, and poppies in beds as if they were flowers in a vase. Cobalt blue delphiniums and artemisias give an English feel to the garden. Near the pond in spring, hundreds of yellow flag iris grow with abandon. All the cottage-style plantings appear loose and casual, but there is a well-planned structure to this garden. As Ann Balusek explains, "We want an organized garden but not an organized look."

The Baluseks consider themselves stewards of their property, and their objective has been to create enticing garden rooms and areas that look like they have been there since the house was built. They have created a captivating English country garden seen through various vignettes, all artfully arranged and meticulously maintained.

Right: In spring, the English-inspired mixed borders adjoining the pergola terrace feature peonies, roses, and poppies, while large drifts of yellow flag iris (*Iris pseudacorus*) across the lawn brighten the edge of the pond.

Right: Spires of cobalt-blue delphiniums contrast with colorful roses, poppies, and chartreuse lady's mantle.

CRAB TREE FARM

LAKE BLUFF

Crab Tree Farm has a distinguished lineage, beginning in 1906 when Grace Garrett Durand established a dairy business on the property. In the mid-1920s, the Durands sold eleven lakefront acres to William McCormick Blair and his wife, Helen, who commissioned a rambling clapboard house from noted architect David Adler, where they summered for sixty years. The late John Bryan and his wife, Neville, purchased the lakefront property in 1984 and, a year later, acquired the Durand farm buildings and land from the Blair family.

The Adler house and the farm buildings designed by Chicago architect Solon S. Beman became the setting for John Bryan's notable collection of Georgian furniture and decorative arts and British and American arts and crafts pieces. Neville Bryan's interest was in the landscape. Together this preservation-minded couple has greatly enhanced Crab Tree Farm, and today it is the last Illinois working farm on Lake Michigan with a breathtaking panorama of gardens, forest, fields, and follies.

In collaboration with Virginia landscape architect Charles Stick, Neville Bryan restored the rose garden that Ellen Biddle Shipman and Adler designed for the Blairs. Today, parterres edged with closely clipped boxwood and filled with pink and yellow roses are enclosed by an informal perimeter planting.

Completing the vista to the west is the Jefferson House, a folly designed by Adler that is a focal point at the end of a forested allée. Over the years, the Bryans added other follies that are nestled among the oak and hickory forest—the English pavilion with its eighteenth-century exterior and interior English moldings, the "little house" built in the style of the main house, the 1840s log cabin, and the thatched hermitage. Classical garden sculpture has been placed along winding grass paths in carefully chosen spots within the chest-high clipped forest understory.

The heart of the gardens at Crab Tree Farm is Neville Bryan's cutting and vegetable garden, which is set against the background of the service court. Bordered on one side by a line of pleached crab apple trees, American bittersweet-covered arches mark the entrances to the garden. Boxwood-edged beds of vegetables, including Neville's southern heritage okra and tomatoes, provide a feast for her and her neighbors' tables.

Above: Crab trees front the Durand dairy farm buildings, which were designed by S. S. Beman after a fire destroyed the original diary complex in 1910.

Opposite: The Jefferson House folly sits at the end of a cathedral-like allée in the forest.

Overleaf: In the rose garden pink and yellow hybrid tea roses fill boxwood-edged parterres while climbing roses, Clematis 'Jackmanii', and ferns hug the perimeter walls.

Flower beds of annuals and perennials are symmetrically positioned, exploding with color in late summer. The flowery beds beautifully complement the various shapes and shades of growing green vegetables.

For his own garden, John Bryan, working with artist Jo Hormuth of Chicago, designed a formal walled garden across the drive from the vegetable and cutting garden. The central lawn is surrounded by perimeter beds of woodland ferns, epimedium, and ligularia while climbing hydrangea vines scamper over the walls. Impressive lead statuary by John Cheere greets the visitor as does a monumental seventeenth-century lead cistern overflowing with sedum.

Adjacent to these gardens is a Georgian-style tennis house built designed by James O'Connor, a New York architect who worked in collaboration with David Adler and Robert Work. This structure was used by the Blair family for winter weekend tennis parties. Today, the ivy wainscoted walls and finials, along with views through open screen doors, provide a green backdrop for tennis matches.

Crab Tree Farm is an extraordinary complex of buildings and gardens, all meticulously maintained. The guiding lights for the last thirty-five years have been the Bryans. Together, graciously and unassumingly, they created an exceptional sense of place.

Right: Neville Bryan's kitchen garden is a combination of perennials, annuals, vegetables, and herbs filling boxwood-edged quadrants.

A complex of colonial-style outbuildings, pleached crab apple trees, and a greenhouse are a handsome backdrop.

Above: The centerpiece of
the walled garden is a large
lead cistern overflowing with
sedum facing a lawn panel.
Surrounding borders are
filled with ferns, epimedium,
ligularia, and hydrangeas
climbing the stone walls.

Top: An entrance to the walled garden from the woodland is seen through white crab apple branches and a carpet of ostrich ferns.

Above: White crab apple trees, narcissus, and ferns surround an antique figure of Spring.

Above: An eighteenth-cen-
tury lead figure of Mercury
by John Cheere stands out-
side the walled garden.

Opposite: In the sky-lit
tennis house, wainscoted
walls are covered in ivy with
espaliered eagles.

Overleaf: A sculpted haw-
thorn frames a view across the
pasture to the summer house
and diary complex.

THE GARDENS AT 900

LAKE FOREST

On Craig Bergmann's fifth birthday, his father
gave him a twenty-by-twenty-foot plot of
land behind the family garage. Over the years,
Craig swapped plants with other gardeners
and tended his garden, even enhancing it with
garden statuary purchased with job earnings.
Bergmann's talents have significantly developed
since then. Today, he leads a thriving landscape
design firm, and his artistry can be seen at the
varied and educational Gardens at 900.

Bergmann and his partner, Paul Klug, an interior
designer, had been searching for some years for
a home to share. Little did they know when Paul
saw a real estate ad in 2009 for the property at
900 North Waukegan Road in Lake Forest that
they would find the perfect place to combine their
professional and personal lives within a handsome
architectural complex.

The property has a fabled history. Elsa and
A. Watson Armour set about in 1915 to create
a gentleman's farm called Elawa Farm, a
combination of his initials and first two letters
of her given name. Two gatehouses and a motor
house designed by architect David Adler and Robert Work were built, but plans
for the main house were abandoned during World War I and the Depression.
When the Armour fortune revived in the early 1930s, the couple decided to
remain in their idyllic compound and forego the manor house.

Landscape architect Ralph Root laid out the garden in 1920. Little remained by
the 2000s so Bergmann sought out vintage photographs for design reference.
The original traditional design and Bergmann's own creations are combined in
a beautiful montage of garden spaces. Bergmann's additions include a parking
grove, entry garden, double borders, shade garden, orchard, and silver garden.

Over twenty years at his garden center, Country Garden in Winthrop Harbor,
Illinois, Bergmann amassed a collection of specimens that he could not leave
behind when he decided to focus exclusively on landscape design. This diverse
group of plants, including fully grown trees, a Belgian fence of espaliered apple

Above: Pink and red bee
balm and lilies surround a
weathered statue.

Opposite: Clematis vines
scramble over the arbor
above a variegated dap-
pled willow (*Salix integra
'Hakuro-Nishiki'*).

trees, old roses and thousands of perennials, account for approximately 90 percent of the principal ingredients in the new garden.

There are two approaches to the Gardens at 900: a formal motor courtyard and an iron gate, supported by two carved stone figures, which leads directly into the garden. The garage complex, which serves as Bergmann's studio offices, is flanked by the gatehouses. One houses Klug's business and the other is their residence. The gravel courtyard is formal in design with boxwood cones, globes, and hedges bordered with Elsa Armour's German iris in spring and Russian sage in summer. Trimmed myrtle and boxwood topiaries add elegant accents.

Bergmann's vision for the property was an English country-style garden. "I wanted to configure the spaces formally but plant them informally," he explains. Today, two formal borders burst forth in vivid hues from spring to fall with peonies, foxgloves, phlox, astilbes, and many other perennials. Throughout the property are design and horticultural vignettes that include antique statuary, ornaments, and containers billowing with unusual plants.

In addition to the floriferous garden rooms, the shade garden and orchard provide calm, naturalistic settings. "The shade garden and orchard are my favorites with their ramshackle planting mixes," Bergmann says. "They have evolved over the years and provide habitats for insects and wildlife—and fun for our trio of Norwich terriers."

Right: The motor court border features royal purple German irises, one of Elsa Armour's favorites.

Overleaf: The west gardens feature double mixed borders planted with day lilies, phlox, hydrangeas, and red dipladinia covering metal obelisks. Tall hornbeam cylinders provide a dramatic background.

Opposite: A snowfall of pink crab apple blossoms appears in spring.

Top: Overflowing containers of blue fan flower (*Scaevola aemula*) animate an inviting dining terrace.

Above: Spires of foxglove accentuate the mixed borders in summer.

Above: A rustic arbor marks a path leading to the oval shade garden, which features brightly colored coleus, chartreuse Japanese forest grass, a golden Japanese maple, and silvery blue heart-shaped brunnera.

KELTON HOUSE FARM

FREDONIA, WISCONSIN

Kelton House is named for the family who built the colonial oak-sided saltbox structure in the 1740s in the Connecticut River Valley. Two hundred and thirty years later, the house was dismantled and carefully moved to Wisconsin. Joe Gromacki, a passionate preservationist and collector of seventeenth- and eighteenth-century colonial American furniture and American and British decorative arts, acquired the property two decades ago. He has devoted much time and effort to create a rural farmstead that features colonial-style gardens filled with heirloom plants. Varieties include both European species brought to the colonies and native American species found in the wild but collected and cultivated domestically centuries ago. There are more than a thousand varieties, many grown from seed, that date to the eighteenth-century or earlier.

Gromacki has designed these gardens as a montage of early American designs and plantings based on research in his extensive library of antiquarian books on American architecture, gardens, and farming. "As in the eighteenth century in America, gardens were often designed by owners, there were no landscape professionals as such," he explains. In contrast to the formality of late seventeenth- and early eighteenth-century European gardens and the romantic English gardens promoted by Capability Brown after the 1750s, the colonists, surrounded by untamed land, opted for gardens ordered through geometry with neatly trimmed hedges and paths, enclosed with a verdant or wooden barrier.

Naturalistic style serpentine borders, luxuriantly planted with heirloom perennials, biennials, herbs, and annuals, frame the lawn in front of the house. Close to the house, a small geometrically designed herb garden boasts an antique finial from Gloucester Cathedral in England. Throughout the farm, Gromacki has skillfully placed antique English and American garden ornaments, including eight English eighteenth-century staddle stones supporting a peafowl house.

Opposite a long entrance lane are "falling" terraced gardens, separated by grassy slopes and paths. This type of garden was popular in colonial America and provided farmers the opportunity to showcase their garden specimens—ornamental, fruit, and vegetable—on these descending terraces. At Kelton House Farm, as in the eighteenth century, the highest "fall" that is closest to the house, contains the rarest plants. Lower terraces were reserved for vegetables.

Above: Peacocks join heritage breeds of cattle, sheep, chickens, geese, and doves on this working farm.

Opposite: An eighteenth-century Scottish thistle finial sits in a bed of sedums in a cutting garden of heirloom annuals and herbs. An antique wrought-iron arbor, found in an Oxford University courtyard, connects to a second cutting garden.

On the upper "fall," heirloom pear trees are carefully trained to grow over the late eighteenth-century wrought-iron arbor that originally graced an inner college courtyard garden at Oxford University. Other espaliered apple and pear trees grow upright against the barn and other dependencies. Cut-flower gardens are filled with daisies, sweet peas, and exotic kiss-me-over-the-garden-gate. The upper cutting and fruit gardens provide spectacular views of the surrounding countryside.

A large manicured boxwood parterre garden takes center stage on the second terrace. The design, based on a seventeenth-century engraving, includes crushed oyster shells as a floor, which provides a striking contrast to the manicured emerald green shrubs. Heirloom vegetable gardens flank the parterre garden. The lowest "fall," with its bounty of vegetables and a massive English seventeenth-century cider press, bursts forth in late summer with cardoons, kales, and globe artichokes, highlighted by colorful *Verbena bonariensis* and heirloom zinnias.

Over the years, Gromacki has expanded the farm from its original forty-five acres to more than two hundred. This has allowed him to develop a moss garden, meadows, woods and a working farm, including heritage breeds of cattle, sheep, chickens, geese, doves, peacocks and, for better or worse, a herd of deer. Kelton House Farm is a house and garden treasure emphasizing the finest in horticulture and colonial American garden design.

Right: Beside the house is an enclosed colonial-style dooryard garden with culinary and medicinal herbs highlighted by myrtle topiaries and a stone finial from Gloucester Cathedral.

Overleaf: A vintage cider
press is the focal point in the
lower vegetable terrace.

Above: The lower vegetable
terrace features artichokes
and drifts of *Verbena bonariensis* while the mezzanine level
garden sports sunflowers.

Top: Near the barn are tripod poles growing hops.

Above: Rustic teepees support heirloom pole beans of the same variety found at Monticello. The border is a trimmed hedge of sage.

Right: A meticulously trimmed boxwood parterre, vegetables, and sunflowers can be seen on the second "fall" with the peafowl house elevated with English staddle stones.

Overleaf: The view from the top "fall" shows the boxwood parterre, the lower vegetable and flower gardens, and the expansive working fields beyond. The parterre design is taken from John Parkinson's *Paradisi in Sole Paradisus Terrestris*, published in 1629.

OLD MILL FARM

LAKE FOREST

Gardening runs in Frank Mariani's blood. His grandfather, John Fiore, established a nursery in Lake Forest in 1915, and his father subsequently migrated the business into a significant residential maintenance operation. Mariani has transformed the family company into a fully integrated landscape design, installation, and maintenance firm. With this background, it is no surprise that he and his wife, Sherri, have created a captivating garden near his grandfather's original property.

The couple bought the 1929 Tudor-style house and ten-acre farm in 1986. Her principal objective was to restore the house while Frank focused on reclaiming the property from invasive species like buckthorn and Norway maple. A pleasant surprise was the discovery in the attic of Jens Jensen's 1934 plans for the property. Few portions of the design were implemented, and only the woodland garden today bears a resemblance to the original Jensen plans.

Next came the lawns, both in front and back, for family activities. Soon afterward, Mariani set about creating his first enclosed garden—an ornamental vegetable and cutting garden. An avid cook, he says, "I wanted my own vegetable garden so I could go out and pick whatever was needed for dinner that night."

Above: Narcissus and daffodils carpet the ground under a grove of birch trees.

Opposite: A pleached pear hedge leads to a rustic arbor adjoining the ornamental kitchen garden.

The vegetable garden is anchored with a handsome pleached pear hedge entrance and fenced with country-style cedar slats. More than three dozen pots filled with flowers and herbs sit on the flagstone entry. Boxwood hedges and globes lend touches of formality, and framed beds of cherry tomatoes scamper on a wooden arbor inspired by the high pitch of the Tudor house. Squash vines creep and artichokes leap while sweet peas, clematis, other ornamentals, and vegetables climb tuteurs, rustic wigwams, and fences.

Once the vegetable garden was established, Mariani embarked on a perennial border near the house. Enclosed on two sides by yew hedges, the romantic border opens onto a spectacular view of the prairie and vegetable garden. Native coneflowers and queen of the prairie mingle with phlox, peonies, and other perennials that furnish color from spring to fall.

In 2004 Mariani began renovating the prairie with the removal of teasel and other non-native plants. The first sowing of prairie seed was in 2007. "Prairies are not easy to establish, but maintaining these special habitats is the major challenge," he explains. More than fifteen species of prairie grasses have taken hold alongside flowering perennials such as spiderwort, purple coneflower, Culver's root, and New England aster, and the overall effect is a dreamy haze that sways with the wind. Bordered by the Lake County Forest Preserves, the wide prairie vista is breathtaking under the expansive sky.

Adjacent to the prairie is a productive orchard filled with fruit and nut trees. Apple trees, some more than twenty-five years old, have been espaliered in a candelabra pattern over an archway while other cordon espaliers stand along the fence.

Over the years, the long drive has been luxuriantly supplemented with various cultivars of hellebores, ferns, narcissus, and leucojums along with redbuds and crab apple trees. Spring is a fairyland of delicate colors and textures. The scene changes in summer with bottlebrush buckeye and hydrangeas in charge. Fall brings a feast of color along the drive.

New gardens are always in progress at Old Mill Farm. The latest is a pond beyond the vegetable garden with a welcoming pergola of weathered silver-gray tree limbs covered with rambling pink roses.

Right: Espaliered fruit trees separate the orchard from the ample lawn and prairie beyond. Adirondack chairs face the house and surrounding gardens.

Overleaf: Squash, beans, tomatoes, and herbs mix with nasturtiums, cosmos, and dahlias in the vegetable garden.

Right: A seemingly endless vista extends out beyond lush perennial borders of soft-colored astilbe, coneflowers, Culver's root, and queen of the prairie (*'Filipendula rubra'*).

TENBROEK GARDEN

LAKE FOREST

Sara and Jim Tenbroek grew up with gardening parents. Sara discovered her love of peonies in Illinois, while Jim, in Minnesota, grew vegetables and fruits, including his favorite—pumpkins. Their love of horticulture led the couple to develop gardens at each place they have lived, and today, in Lake Forest.

While their Georgian revival house was being restored, the Tenbroeks considered the grounds. Seeking plans for a garden with "some patina" by the time they moved in, they chose Craig Bergmann as their landscape architect because, as Sara says, "his approach was painterly and romantic."

Today, resplendent in spring, two white-flowering crab apple trees anchor the gravel entrance drive and frame the ivy-clad house along with simple but elegant boxwood plantings. They were planted in honor of Grace Durand's Crab Tree Farm, which was on this site before moving to Lake Bluff.

Above: The crescent-shaped rose garden is framed by Annabelle hydrangeas.

Opposite: A cloud of crab apple blossoms highlights the formal ivy-clad entrance in spring.

Bergmann created two gardens near the house—a formal garden and a terrace garden. For the formal garden, he installed a double hedge along the west wall of white-flowering *Heptacodium* or Seven Sons Tree interspersed with crab apples and tall Adam's columnar yews facing the garden. A bubbling fountain with plantings of towering white meadow rue on either side, together with the green hedge wall, softens the sounds of passing traffic. The garden is laid out with brick-edged beds of perennials and roses. Blue delphiniums and foxgloves are the soaring stars, surrounded by catmint, daisies, and roses. Sara's beloved peonies are planted along the edges of many beds.

Set between the two wings of the house, the bluestone terrace is the family gathering place in the summer. Bergmann suggested planting pear whips on the two walls between the French doors for viewing while on the terrace or from the kitchen window. Today espaliers bearing fruit ascend to the roof's edge. Small beds of roses and perennials sit on different levels within the bluestone masonry, and lead planters hold Meyer lemon trees. The view from the terrace extends across a large greensward to a graceful crescent rose garden surrounding an urn and bordered by billowing Annabelle hydrangeas.

The couple inherited a cutting and vegetable garden, which they expanded into a place for their young twin daughters to learn about nature. This garden includes butterfly-attracting flowers, such as zinnias, as well as vegetables, herbs, and fruit for the house. But more importantly, it is a laboratory for the children to observe the transformation of seeds to seedlings to plants to harvest. And, of course, they have pumpkins, although Sara says, "not enough for all Halloween activities."

Right: Tall meadow rue (*Thalictrum 'Elin'*) near the fountain presides over the formal garden with beds of roses, delphiniums, foxgloves, lilies, catmint, and peonies.

Above: Espaliered pear trees, which bear fruit in late summer, complement the bluestone terrace garden with its boxwood-edged beds of roses and perennials.

Top: Spires of apricot-colored foxglove rise from a lead planter. Pig-squeak (*Bergenia*) offers a layer of glossy leaves under the crab apple tree.

Above: In late summer, the bounty of the kitchen garden includes zinnias, dahlias, vegetables, herbs, and pears.

LENHARDT GARDEN

WINNETKA

When my wife, Cindy, and I purchased our Nantucket-style house forty years ago, there was not much of a garden. Having been bitten by the gardening bug in my grandparents' garden when I was ten years old, I finally had the opportunity to continue "digging in the dirt." I had no overall plan for the garden and instead relied on trial and error and many garden visits with the Garden Conservancy for inspiration. The house architecture, the work of Edwin Clark in 1916, and its site at the top of one of the southernmost ravines on the North Shore guided all my decisions.

My first challenge was the front garden. A colonial-style cedar fence once surrounded the property, but by the time we took ownership, most of the fence in front had fallen down. The house and garden could breathe, and a view opened onto the road. Today, guests are greeted by lushly planted window boxes and planters filled with geraniums and petunias, a Nantucket staple. Large sculptured beds of pachysandra, punctuated with boxwood and yew globes, anchor the setting.

Above: Window boxes and urns overflow with pink geraniums and annuals while New Dawn climbing roses and white clematis scamper up a trellis.

Opposite: Mixed terrace borders filled with goose-neck loosestrife (*Lysimachia clethroides*), purple loosestrife (*Lythrum salicaria*), queen of the prairie (*Filipendula rubra*), and roses give way to ravine and knot gardens in the distance.

A shrub border, set off by the old fence, leads to the rear garden. Cornelian-cherry dogwood, witch hazel, Wentworth viburnum, and false spirea mingle with beds of variegated dogwood and white astilbe along the border. Three legacy oak trees offer a canopy for this tranquil setting. Climbing hydrangeas scale up two of the heritage oaks.

The focal points looking east include a boxwood parterre and ravine garden. The parterre, a nod to my southern heritage, with urns filled with flax lily and white dead-nettles, is embraced by double hedges of yew and arrowwood viburnum. Hostas—of different colors, variegation and sizes—ferns, and ground covers intermingle with oakleaf hydrangeas and shrubs in the woodland background.

The ravine garden is a more recent project, and I have Frank Cabot, founder of the Garden Conservancy, to thank for inspiration. His deep ravine setting at Quatre Vents introduced me to large-leafed butterbur, rodgersia, and other dramatic specimens. Conditions vary dramatically—flooding with spring rain and parched earth in August heat, all in shade—and only a limited number of plants can thrive. Water-loving Siberian and Japanese iris bloom in early June, and as the summer continues, great blue lobelia and Joe Pye weed put on a show. Playing a leading role is large-leafed butterbur. Today the ravine flourishes with plants of different textures, shapes, heights and shades of green.

From a neighboring bridge, there is a view of our terraced borders set into the rolling hillside and separated by hand-laid fieldstone walls. Perennials in shades of blue, purple and pink, with dashes of white and an assortment of annuals, give seasonal color. Two self-seeders are my favorites—*Verbena bonariensis*, which blooms wherever it wishes and provides a haze of lavender, and feverfew, a flower that grew in my grandmother's garden. A bed of pink shrub roses, interspersed with sedum and catmint, hugs the slope.

Our living and dining rooms open onto a large screened terrace, the perfect place to sit and view the garden. Trellises on both corners feature white clematis and 'New Dawn' roses that put on a mid-summer show while a small boxwood-edged garden filled with the fragrant Scepter'd Isle rose plays a supporting role.

Right: The ravine garden includes giant Japanese butterbur (*Petatsites japonicus*), Joe Pye weed, Siberian and Japanese irises, variegated sweet flag, and ferns.

Above: Caesar's Brother
Siberian iris and giant
Japanese butterbur thrive in
the moist soil of the ravine
adjoining the woodland
garden.

Top: The shrub border is
punctuated with white astilbe
and variegated dogwood
while climbing hydrangeas
clamber up the oak trees.

Above: The knot garden has
a double-tiered boxwood
topiary center surrounded by
white begonias. Variegated
flax lilies and spotted dead-
nettle fill the urns.

Top: Stone steps descend through the terrace borders, which are filled with soft-colored perennials and annuals.

Above: In late summer, white Culver's root and Joe Pye weed put on a show in the upper terrace border.

Opposite: Globe amaranth (*Gomphrena globosa 'Fireworks'*), sedums, Russian sage, cat-mint, coneflower, phlox, and spider flowers blend together on the hillside.

NATURALISTIC GARDENS

LEVIN GARDEN

HIGHLAND PARK

Thirty years ago, Don Levin, a devoted conservationist, enlisted landscape architect Scott Byron to save and restore fourteen acres of abandoned farmland. The two continue to "let the land give them direction" as they carry on enhancing this unique Midwest sanctuary.

The story began when Levin and his wife, Kathy, purchased one of the few remaining large undeveloped tracts on the North Shore. The farm had not been tended for forty years, so invasive buckthorn dominated ten acres, with savanna oaks on the remaining property. Byron's objective was to fulfill the Levins' mission to be good stewards of the land and, at the same time, add beautiful and unexpected elements to the landscape.

In keeping with the goal of restoration, the more formal gardens are near the house and pool house where boxwood hedges and globes provide order amid occasional splashes of seasonal color. To the west of the front entrance, a lichen-covered pergola opens onto emerald-green grass, which is encircled by a low irregular stone wall, antique sundial, and annuals. After clearing almost two acres of buckthorn near the house, two ponds, with native plantings to their edge, were developed and also act as irrigation for the gardens. These gardens, which can be seen from the house, are a prelude to the naturalistic scenes further afield.

Above: Chicago-area native, cockspur hawthorn (*Crataegus crus-galli*) blooms in spring.

Opposite: Bald cypress trees and white-flowering hawthorn trees line the entrance drive.

Overleaf: Crab apple trees mark a meadow opening with hawthorns beyond.

With a nod to O. C. Simonds, legendary Midwest landscape gardener, Byron has created a series of landscape pictures based on two and one half miles of interconnecting curvilinear pathways and undulating planting patterns filled with indigenous trees, shrubs, and flowers. Disappearing sandy gravel paths through groves of white pine, hemlock, and maples offer an enticement to explore. "The sky is celebrated," Byron says, as wooded walkways suddenly open up to a prairie.

The centerpiece of the apple orchard, with its alpine currant hedge, is the slatted pergola with its climbing wisteria and plantings of Annabelle hydrangea, astilbe, and turtlehead, all adding summer color to this mostly native plant palette. A gently sloping maple allée leads from the orchard to an impressive climbing hydrangea arch before entering the pool house terrace. Weathered pergolas, oversized wooden gates and doorways, along with secluded benches, in strategic sites throughout the property, offer enchanting vistas.

It is magical to walk along these dappled shade
serpentine passages surrounded by Cornelian dogwood
and crab apple tree canopies with carpets below of
ostrich ferns, Queen Anne's lace, bee balm, and other
perennials. Miraculously, the calm from these shady
groves can be suddenly shattered as the path opens up
onto a sunny field of grasses and goldenrod swaying in
the wind and shimmering as they twist.

Above, left: Wild phlox and
other native perennials grow
along sandy gravel pathways.

Above: Climbing hydrangea
hugs a large wooden gate that
opens onto the apple orchard.

Right: A weathered arbor entwined with climbing hydrangea marks the beginning of the maple allée leading to the orchard.

Overleaf: Bordered by sweeping soft-colored perennials and annuals, the pond is a refuge for birds and other wildlife.

MARY ANN'S GARDEN

METTAWA

A diverse and significant Asian sculpture collection assembled by Barry MacLean was the impetus for his late wife, Mary Ann, to create her garden in the early 1990s. Landscape architect Craig Bergmann assisted with the design of "floating islands" in a naturalized setting amid a Midwest forest with strategically placed sculptures and other antiquities. Bold plantings, to balance the large carved and cast forms, were placed in island beds among expanses of turf and along the forest perimeter. The striking plant combinations act as a counterpoint to nature's random placement of massive white oaks and sugar maples. Linking the various beds are paths of slate imported from Shandong province in China and paths edged with Indiana limestone.

Above: A Ming dynasty general stands behind a Tang dynasty horse.

Opposite: A replica of a Ming dynasty seated Buddha is surrounded by hosta and white-blooming false spirea (*Sorbaria sorbifolia*).

Overleaf: Chinese horses in the sugar maple and white oak forest in autumn.

The extraordinary stone sculptures date from the fourteenth to eighteenth century, some massive, such as a pair of Qing Dynasty standing horses and the Ming Dynasty columns, and others smaller such as dynastic brass bells, iron cisterns, and stone stools. Many had religious or ritual functions and are often decorated with botanical and animal motifs that enhance their meaning beyond pure function.

Mary Ann MacLean was not timid in her choice of flower and leaf colors for the garden. Red, orange, and yellow, combined with purples and occasionally pink, have been artistically arranged to amplify the beauty of the sculptures. The topography of plantings has been considered since a plant too tall will obscure a vista and change the balance; with an eye to controlling maintenance, the plants mostly tend themselves.

In early spring the garden is bathed in drifts of narcissus, hellebores, and leucojum under limbs of oriental cherry trees. Summer follows with peonies, astilbes, alliums, and hostas. Impressive stands of Joe Pye weed transition into the forest. Throughout the growing season beautiful Japanese maples lend lovely shades of red, orange, and yellow. Bronze and cast-iron antique containers are planted with colorful seasonal annuals and perennials. Bluestone gravel trails, near the forest's edge, wind among queen of the prairie, cup plants, and woodland sunflowers. When autumn approaches, the garden transitions into its fall dress with tall grasses and trees with bronze, yellow, orange, and red leaves.

Mary Ann's garden has a spirit of adventure at every
twist and turn, revealing beautiful native species and
monumental ancient sculptures. At the same time, it
is a place for reflection and appreciation of the natural
beauty of the Midwest.

Above, left: Dusty pink blossoms of queen of the prairie complement the elegant Ming dynasty stone temple structure beyond.

Above and overleaf: A zig-zag gravel path moves through the lawn to the elevated stone temple.

Above: A pair of marble Ming dynasty columns in the meadow in late summer.

Above, right: Autumn grasses surround iron and bronze bells from China and Southeast Asia, which range in date from the sixteenth to nineteenth century.

THE SECRET GARDEN

LAKE FOREST

After living in France for four years, Jean Greene and her late husband, John, returned to Lake Forest in 1963 and purchased a distinctive 1923 Mediterranean-style house with a walled garden, known to neighborhood children as the "secret garden."

Living in Europe had a profound influence on the garden's development—Jean and John wanted to change the traditional rectangular garden they had inherited to something more natural. The stars were aligned when John, a long-standing board member of the Chicago Botanic Garden, met the late John Brookes, prominent English landscape architect, in 1991 while Brookes was designing the Helen and Richard Thomas English Walled Garden at the Botanic Garden. Brookes suggested that the Greenes enlist Chicago landscape architect Doug Hoerr for the assignment as Doug had just completed an internship with him in England. Doug was eager to demonstrate his skills on the project, his first major residential commission since returning from England and the founding of his practice in Chicago.

Above: A curving path underneath a pair of Japanese maples invites discovery.

Opposite: In spring, this perennial bed hosts irises, alliums, astilbes, and roses.

Hoerr created a garden that feels much larger than it is by dividing the property into distinct areas—lawn, woodland, pond, flower beds, and entryway gardens. The emerald-green carpet, which abuts shallow semicircular steps, is the central area from which other gardens radiate. The influence of Beth Chatto—British plantswoman, garden designer, and author, with whom Hoerr also apprenticed—is evident in various plants growing randomly through the gravel terrace.

The woodland walk is devoted primarily to native Illinois wildflowers and plants that thrive in the shade. This spot includes one of John's favorite plants, butterbur (*Petasites japonicus*), the giant leaf perennial that grows wild along the streams in Claude Monet's garden at Giverny and can survive the North Shore winters. The entire walled area is enclosed with large conifers, Japanese maples, and magnolias.

Throughout the garden, whimsical bronze sculptures of animals—foxes, otters, frogs, and grasshoppers by Jean Greene, a sculptress and painter—give a sense of humor and surprise to the garden. The curved pond is edged with handsome weathered seamface Wisconsin boulders selected jointly at the quarry by Jean and Hoerr. The stones also act as pedestals for bronzes such as *Ballet Dreamer*, a lively frog who lifts a foot in delight near the pond. Jean says, "John posed for this sculpture."

Close to Jean's studio is John's small prairie garden. This area contains Joe Pye weed, wild phlox, goldenrod, fall-blooming anemone, and cup plants *(Silphium perfoliatum)*. John, an ardent conservationist, was always proud to show his towering cup plants, whose leaves form cups where they join the stem. Water collects in the "cups" and birds often drink from them. The plants can grow ten feet tall and are among the tallest flora found on the Illinois prairie. John's other loves were his raised vegetable beds and beehives. A long-time beekeeper, John was delighted with Hoerr's choice of shrubs, perennials, and annuals as they are hosts for many pollinators buzzing about the garden.

Right: Shallow steps, with lady's mantle, lamb's ear, and other perennials growing out of the gravel treads, descend from the terrace to the lawn and the pond.

Top: Secluded seating beside the lawn.

Above: Goldenrod, Joe Pye weed, phlox, and cup plant (*Silphium perfoliatum*) in late-summer bloom.

Above: A spring-blooming
pagoda dogwood stands
beside raised vegetables beds.

Above and opposite: Jean
Greene's bronze sculptures
are installed at the edge of the
pond amid yellow iris and
buttercups. A woodland
walk features native ground
covers and ornamental
shade-loving perennials.

WILLIAMS-BECKER GARDEN

GLENCOE

This garden combines a Jens Jensen-inspired meadow of prairie and wildflower plantings with a "Japanesque" landscape that reflects the deep interest that Nicole Williams and Larry Becker share in Asian art and culture. They have traveled extensively in Japan, visiting gardens there whenever possible. The Japanesque gardens are close to the house, easily seen from the expansive windows of the contemporary building. Further from their oriental pavilion is the meadow, an homage to Jensen, who worked on the property in 1903 as his first residential project and returned in 1914.

"Trees are our number one priority in the garden," Williams observes. Together, the couple has assembled a significant collection of Japanese maples, rare shrubs, and trees. Today the garden contains over fifty cultivars of maples ranging in height from three to ten feet with foliage that ranges from deep burgundy to brilliant chartreuse. Throughout the growing season, Becker prunes all of them as well as the conifers and even a low-lying horizontal beech. His handiwork can be seen on weeping, cascading, and upright forms.

The small entrance courtyard is a peaceful and inviting arrival space. Specimen conifers, Japanese maples, and other deciduous trees soften the stark lines of the architecture. To the right of the doorway, a path leads to a Japanese gateway that opens onto a mystical shade garden overlooking a steep ravine. The spectacular foliage of Japanese maples is present from early spring to late autumn both here and in other parts of the garden.

On the other side of the house is a veranda, or *engawa* in Japanese, that complements the Asian character of the house and enhances the connection with the garden. A majestic white pine, underplanted with dwarf coniferous shrubs and Japanese maples, dominates this area. A raked rectangle gravel garden was developed to suggest ocean waves and cliffs. Becker found some of Jens Jensen's faux rocks on the site. These are now moss-covered and used as edging for the gravel garden. Slightly further from the house, a small stream flows over a waterfall into a water lily pond full of Japanese goldfish and koi. Overlooking this area is a Japanese teahouse and bridge that traverses a dry creek bed planted with iris, large hostas, and bald cypress trees.

Above: A shady path with ferns, conifers, and Japanese maples overlooks a steep ravine.

Opposite: Japanese painted ferns and Japanese maples of different colors and sizes line the path to the *torii* gateway to a shade garden.

Overleaf: The central lawn is surrounded with limestone wedges arranged with outcroppings of perennials and conifers. Atop the raised platform are rare Japanese maple cultivars and evergreens.

In the upper garden, spring is aglow with yellow magnolias, pink dogwoods, American cherries, serviceberries, and viburnums. Adding interest is the stone terrace around the old estate guest house, along with the original well-nourished foundation plantings and stonework by Jensen. While developing the garden, Williams and Becker reinforced the slope with massive Wisconsin limestone outcroppings with conifers and perennials tucked among the stones. Summer brings many perennial blooms, including Joe Pye weed, astilbes, native wildflowers, and prairie grasses. These plantings provide a contrast to the Japanesque garden elements near the house.

This husband-and-wife team has masterfully created gardens that respect the terrain's heritage and Jensen's contributions, and at the same time, show their intense love and care for trees, especially Japanese maples.

Right: A canary-yellow flowered magnolia (*Magnolia acuminata*) and the russet leaves of a Japanese maple are harbingers of early spring.

Above and opposite: Chinese yellow Bartzella Itoh peonies and white astilbe offer subtle spring color; coneflowers, ornamental alliums, astilbes, hyssops (*Agastache foeniculum 'Blue Fortune'*), and bear's breeches (*Acanthus mollis*) create bold drifts of color in full summer.

Above: Conifers and Japanese
maples are carefully placed to
offer color and contrast.

Top: A blue spruce (*Picea pungens* 'Ruby Teardrops') with wine-colored tips coordinates hue with the Japanese maples.

Above: Yellow flag iris bloom in the dry creek bed near the moon bridge.

THE RUMSEY ESTATE

LAKE FOREST

Jens Jensen created gardens for Henry Rumsey in 1913, shortly after the English-style manor house was built to designs by architect Charles Coolidge of Boston. This grand Georgian revival house, modeled after Clifford Manor, a mid-1700s English country house, was home to the Rumseys until the Depression. Afterward, the estate changed hands several times before it was acquired in 2004 by Sandy and Roger Deromedi, who have restored both the house and garden to their original glory.

In preparation, the Deromedis consulted Jensen's landscape plans, housed in his archive at the University of Michigan, and selected Ryan Kettlecamp, a Jensen scholar, and his wife, Claire as landscape architects. Although the drawings showed natural plantings throughout the property, little remained of Jensen's design around the house. Instead, the Deromedis decided to create an English picturesque-style garden near the house, consistent with the style at Clifford Manor.

Elegant boxwood-edged double parterres with seasonal plantings were designed for the front entrance. Facing the rear terrace, a lush perennial border overlooks the lawn with majestic Norway spruces as the background. A koi pond, viewing circle, and grotto can be seen near the front woodland. In keeping with the Jensen plans, winding paths weave their way through planted native trees and shrubs.

A clearing, in the Jensen style, affords a view of the double parterre and house. This meadow shimmers in the sunlight in late summer with its carpet of native sedges and prairie perennials, including the brilliant giant blue lobelia. The landscape is continually changing, and, as Sandy Deromedi says, "We frequently take 'wine walks' in the early evening, strolling to see what's new on the tableland and in the ravine."

The Mayflower Ravine was a significant element in Jensen's original design for the property. Over the past century about 800 feet of ravine had significantly eroded from water run-off, resulting in fallen trees, scoured slopes, and collapsed

Above: A tiered antique fountain complements the formal English-style viewing garden near the house.

Opposite: Giant blue lobelia (*Lobelia siphilitica*) blooms in the clearing of native grasses and prairie perennials that evokes the work of Jens Jensen.

tableland. As Roger says, "It took nature 14,000 years to cut a 25-foot deep ravine, but man's excess water run-off cut an additional five feet in 100 years."

Engineered ravine remediations are typically unaesthetic, and native plantings are generally not used. Here a completely natural look was the goal, with the ability to endure occasional four-foot flash floods that occurred during storm events. The project became an astounding five-year engineering undertaking managed by Roger Deromedi with the assistance of Kettlecamp & Kettlecamp, Rocco Fiore & Sons (landscape restoration), and John Keno & Company (construction).

The slopes were stabilized with buried rock-filled gabion baskets; the streambed was raised using natural stone and boulders; catch basins were installed along the tableland; a dissipation pond was built; and the hillsides were replanted with native species. More than ten million pounds of rock and boulders were imported and selectively placed by Roger and the Keno crew along the streambed to create the desired natural look. More than one million pounds of topsoil was spread, and native plantings of more than 275 trees, 3,400 shrubs and 39,000 perennials were installed. Pathways and dry-stacked limestone walls and steps in the ravine were built to match Jensen's original designs. There are scenic lookout points for appreciating the natural splendor stretching out below, along with a recreated Jensen-style council ring.

In recognition of the Deromedis' stewardship of the original Jensen landscape, the couple received a Lake Forest Preservation Foundation Preservation Award. Today, the Rumsey Estate offers woodland walks, formal parterres, colorful flower borders, and a fascinating ravine excursion.

Above: The restored Jensen
design for the Mayflower
Ravine includes stone steps,
gravel paths, and seating
areas and lookouts, including
a council ring recreated in
the Jensen style.

Above: The motor court features double boxwood-edged parterres with seasonal plantings and urns filled with trailing flowers.

Top: A formal garden near
the house showcases crab
apple trees anchored in
boxwood-enclosed rect-
angles and urns filled with
tropical plants.

Above: Cool colors dominate
the lush English-style perennial border.

Overleaf: The restored
Mayflower Ravine is a defin-
ing feature of the landscape.
Autumn brings gold, char-
treuse, and green foliage to
the steep slopes above the
streambed.

CHICAGO BOTANIC GARDEN

GLENCOE

The Chicago Botanic Garden traces its origin back to the Chicago Horticultural Society, which was founded in 1890. The Society's modern history began in 1965 with the initiation of a new public garden, which opened in 1972. The planners, John O. Simonds and Geoffrey Rausch, were inspired by the famous "Garden of Perfect Brightness," a water garden that once flourished as the Emperor's garden near Beijing. Today the Garden is uniquely sited on 385 acres on and around nine islands, bordered by the splendor of native Midwestern woodlands, the prairie, and a river.

What distinguishes the Garden from other world-class botanic gardens, says Jean Franczyk, President and CEO, is "our emphasis on outstanding design." Over the years, many noted landscape architects and designers, including John Brookes, Scott Byron, Doug Hoerr, Dan Kiley, Mikyoung Kim, Peter Morrow Meyer, Dr. Koichi Kawana, James van Sweden, Michael Van Valkenburgh, and Peter Wirtz, have created gardens.

Within the Garden are twenty-eight display gardens, each of which has a distinct character. Eight are represented here.

Opposite: The iconic linden allée is punctuated by stone spheres.

Above: The Helen and Richard Thomas English Walled Garden melds formal structure with informal cottage-style plantings.

FRANCES C. SEARLE COURTYARD AND MARY WITHERS RUNNELLS COURTYARD

Peter Morrow Meyer designed the courtyards to present the bonsai collection, which was established in 1978 and enhanced in 2000 by a gift of nineteen exquisite specimens from Japanese bonsai master Susumu Nakamura. These living works of art, perfectly positioned on granite benches, feature jasmine, bougainvillea, beech and many varieties of pine. Up to sixty trees can be viewed at once—remarkable by day, breathtaking at night—from May to November.

REGENSTEIN FRUIT & VEGETABLE GARDEN

"Joyful abundance" describes this garden. Growing healthy plants that produce eye-catching, delicious food crosses all boundaries, embraces all nationalities and age groups, and speaks directly to the Midwestern heritage. Five hundred varieties of food crops are grown on four acres—from berries to nuts, herbs to apples and vegetables to grains. Lettuce cascades from hanging baskets, grapevines become part of the architecture, and gorgeous garden display beds are composed entirely of edible flowers, vegetables, and herbs.

CIRCLE GARDEN

Contained within a large circle are inspirational displays of flowering annuals at their most exuberant. Evergreens, boxwood parterres, and yew hedges are the solid green backdrops to brilliant annual color through three seasons. This space contains surprises—two secret gardens on either side of the central fountain are ideal spots for dreaming. Wide brick paths, clipped topiaries, and massed plantings emphasize the formality of the space, while playful water jets, arching grasses and bountiful annuals spilling onto walkways offer a more relaxed garden style.

HELEN AND RICHARD THOMAS
ENGLISH WALLED GARDEN

Enclosed by protective brick walls are charming, intimate garden rooms designed by the late British landscape designer John Brookes. Each room represents a different tradition from England's long gardening history. A wisteria-covered pergola garden, promenade, checkerboard garden, formal daisy garden, perennial border, and cottage garden are focal points. The very formal design is planted with a lush "English muddle" of herbs, bulbs, perennials, annuals and flowering shrubs and trees.

ELIZABETH HUBERT MALOTT
JAPANESE GARDEN

The Garden of Three Islands is a place of beauty and
tranquility designed by Dr. Koichi Kawana. This stroll
garden, with its curving paths curve and stone lanterns,
allows the landscape's inherent beauty, whether on
the ground or across the water, to be slowly revealed.
Plants are tightly pruned to complement hard, craggy
rocks or imitate tree-covered hillsides.

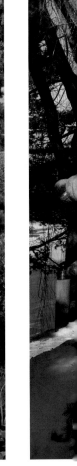

ENGLISH OAK MEADOW

Nestled between the high elevations of the Dwarf Conifer Garden and the rooms of the English Walled Garden is a companion English garden space—a flowering hillside meadow filled with annual flowers and oak trees. The crushed granite walkway cuts a path through the slope, curving toward the Great Basin, offering stunning views of Evening Island and the gardens to the west.

NATURE PLAY GARDEN

The Nature Play Garden, designed for children, features a series of multisensory areas designed by Mikyoung Kim. An expansive lawn that encompasses a runnel, rolling hills, willow tunnel, boulders for climbing, and natural "rooms" defined by arborvitae and hornbeams is surrounded by sugar maples, aspens, and redbud groves.

EVENING ISLAND

Designed by Oehme, van Sweden & Associates, who championed the New American Garden style, Evening Island blends carefully designed walls, terraces and other hardscape features with layered masses of foliage and flowering plants chosen for their ease of maintenance and year-round beauty. This five-acre garden is a living tapestry of texture and color, with grand sweeps of flowering plants and grasses.

ACKNOWLEDGMENTS

Publishing a book, I have learned, involves a family of contributors.

Each of the owners, who so generously opened their beautiful gardens, made this book possible. Not only did they spend time discussing their vision and development of their paradises, they enthusiastically welcomed Scott Shigley and me to their gardens. One of the first rewards of this endeavor was visiting with gardening friends again and meeting new gardening aficionados. Thanks also go to Jean Franczyk and Fred Spicer of the Chicago Botanic Garden for suggesting highlights of this world-class botanic garden.

Noted landscape designers Craig Bergmann, Scott Byron, Doug Hoerr, Claire and Ryan Kettlekamp, Deborah Nevins, and Charles Stick provided advice and counsel. Lois Sheridan coordinated everything at Camp Rosemary, and Marya Padour, head gardener, made sure every garden room was perfect. Tom Gleason at Crab Tree Farm opened doors and windows for us literally. Richard Pegg knew all about the MacLean Collection of Asian art and about plantings as well, while Russ Buvala of Craig Bergmann Landscape Design ensured they looked their best. Nina Koziol was invaluable with her edits and captions assistance.

Barb Carr, a friend and horticultural leader, has kindly written the foreword. Elizabeth White at The Monacelli Press had confidence in me from the beginning, and she kept me on the right track with an editorial process that was iterative, efficient, and pleasant. Susan Evans of Design per se produced the beautiful book design.

This book would not have become a reality without Scott Shigley. Scott, a talented and creative photographic artist, has captured the beauty and atmosphere of each of the gardens. And, equally important, he has become my friend.

Over the last three years, my constant champion and dearest companion has been my wife, Cindy. Not only has she for many years tromped with me through hundreds of gardens around the globe, but she has enthusiastically supported this project and my gardening passion.

The Garden Conservancy is the recipient of all royalties from this publication.

Library of Congress Control Number 2020937603
ISBN 9781580935319

Captions

Page 1: Camp Rosemary
Page 2: Garden Hybrid
Page 4: Beauty Without Boundaries
Pages 12-13: Camp Rosemary
Pages 92-93: Bluhm Garden
Pages 120-121: Crab Tree Farm
Pages 196-197: Levin Garden

Design: Susan Evans, Design per se

Printed in China

The Monacelli Press
65 Bleecker Street
New York, New York 10012